Nutshells

Revision Guide 1991

GW00602749

AUSTRALIA
The Law Book Company Ltd.
Sydney

CANADA
The Carswell Company
Toronto, Ontario

INDIA
N. M. Tripathi (Private) Ltd.
Bombay

Eastern Law House Private Ltd.
Calcutta

M.P.P. House
Bangalore

Universal Book Traders
Delhi

ISRAEL
Steimatzky's Agency Ltd.
Tel Aviv

PAKISTAN
Pakistan Law House
Karachi

Nutshells

Revision Guide 1991

Editors
Leslie Rutherford and Sheila Bone

Contributors

Sheila Bone

Chris Burke

Bob Cooper

Dave Cowley

Greer Hogan

David Howarth

Pat Martin-Moran

Leslie Rutherford

Ralph Tiernan

Steve Wilson

Mick Woodley

Members of the staff, Department of Law,

Newcastle upon Tyne Polytechnic

London   •   Sweet & Maxwell   •   1991

Published in 1991 by Sweet & Maxwell Limited of
South Quay Plaza, 183 Marsh Wall, London E14 9FT
Laserset by P.B. Computer Typesetting,
Pickering, N. Yorks.
Printed by Richard Clay Ltd., Bungay, Suffolk

A CIP catalogue record
for this book is available
from the British Library

Contents

TABLE OF ITEMS INCLUDED

Other Items

CHAPTER 1

COMPANY LAW

CORPORATE PERSONALITY—LIFTING THE VEIL

The facts of the "interesting but exceptionally difficult case" of
ADAMS v. *CAPE INDUSTRIES PLC* [1990] 2 W.L.R. 657 were
complex but gave rise (*inter alia*) to a consideration, by the Court of
Appeal, of one of the core areas of company law, namely corporate
personality and the veil of incorporation. In brief, the defendant
company, Cape Industries plc (Cape), headed a group of companies
involved in the mining of asbestos and the marketing of it worldwide,
including the United States. During the 1970s employees of an
American factory which had processed asbestos supplied by the Cape
group had commenced actions in the United States against a variety
of defendants, including Cape. Those actions never came to trial but
were settled. Cape, without accepting liability or recognising the
jurisdiction of the court, had decided to join in that settlement.
Unfortunately for Cape the matter did not rest there. A further 206
actions were commenced. This time Cape decided upon a different
strategy. As the company had no assets in the United States it
determined to allow default judgments to be obtained against itself
and to defend any subsequent actions in this country for enforcement
of those judgments on the ground that, under the law of this country,
the American court had no jurisdiction over it. On this occasion that
strategy proved successful. Mr Justice Scott dismissed the plaintiffs
actions for enforcement and the Court of Appeal rejected their
appeal.

Present interest lies in the approach taken by the Appeal Court to
what Lord Justice Slade described in his judgment as the "single
economic unit" argument and the "corporate veil" point, two issues
with which students of company law should by this stage of their
studies be fully cognizant. The plaintiffs sought to establish the
necessary presence of Cape within the American court's jurisdiction
by virtue of the presence of its subsidiaries. To do this they had to
establish either that the Cape group of companies should be treated
as one unit or that the corporate veil around these subsidiaries should

1

be lifted so as to view the shareholder who stood behind it, namely Cape.

Counsel for the plaintiffs referred to a number of authorities on the issue of single economic unit including *The Roberta* (1937) 58 L1 L.R. 159, *Harold Holdsworth & Company (Wakefield) Limited* v. *Caddies* [1955] 1 W.L.R. 352, *Scottish Co-operative Wholesale Society Limited* v. *Meyer* [1959] A.C. 324 and *D.H.N. Food Distributors Limited* v. *Tower Hamlets L.B.C.* [1976] 1 W.L.R. 852. In reliance upon these cases it was submitted that in deciding whether a company had rendered itself subject to the jurisdiction of a foreign court it was entirely reasonable to approach the question by reference to "commercial reality." The risk of litigation in a foreign court, it was argued, was part of the price which those who conducted extensive business activities within the territorial jurisdiction of that court properly had to pay. Whilst expressing some sympathy with this argument, Lord Justice Slade stated that in the cases cited above the treatment of parent and subsidiary as one unit, at least for some purposes, could be explained by the wording of a particular statute or contract. Indeed, even the discredited *D.H.N.* case was explicable in those terms. However, his Lordship did not accept counsel's further submission that the theme of all the cited cases was that where legal technicalities would produce injustice in cases involving members of a group of companies, such technicalities should not be allowed to prevail. In Slade L.J.'s view the court was not free to disregard the principle of Salomon merely because it considered that justice so required. Nor was there any general principle that all the companies in a group of companies were to be regarded as one. Moreover, a company was entitled to arrange the affairs of its group in such a way that the business carried on in a particular foreign country was the business of its subsidiary and not its own. On the facts of the present case this was what Cape had done.

The plaintiffs alternative line of attack was that the court should be prepared to lift the corporate veil. In *Woolfson* v. *Strathclyde Regional Council* (1978) 38 P. & C.R. 521 Lord Keith of Kinkel had stated that it was appropriate to pierce the corporate veil only where special circumstances existed indicating that it was a mere facade concealing the true facts.

It was alleged by the plaintiffs that the dissolution of its existing subsidiary and the formation of new companies after the original trial settlement was "a device or sham or cloak for grave impropriety" on the part of the Cape group, namely to ostensibly remove their assets from the United States to avoid liability for asbestos claims whilst at the same time continuing to trade in asbestos there. The allegations of impropriety were subsequently abandoned but the basic intention, namely to continue trading whilst reducing liability, was accepted. But was this sufficient to justify the piercing of the corporate veil? Lord Justice Slade thought not. He did not believe that the court was entitled to lift the corporate veil as against a defendant company which was the member of a corporate group merely because the corporate structure had been used so as to ensure that the legal liability (if any) in respect of particular future activities would fall on another member of the group rather than the defendant company. Such a practice might not be desirable but, according to Slade L.J., the right to use a corporate structure in this manner was inherent in our corporate law. Cape was entitled to organise the group's affairs in that mode and to expect the court to apply the Salomon principle in the ordinary way.

What light, if any, was thrown on the circumstances in which the court will pierce the veil? Unfortunately for the eager examinee, the answer is very little. Like the House of Lords in *Woolfson*, the Court of Appeal elected to hide behind its own veil. Lord Justice Slade was content to state that the authorities cited (for example, *Jones* v. *Lipman* [1962] 1 W.L.R. 832 and "certain broad dicta of Lord Denning M.R." in *Wallersteiner* v. *Moir* [1974] 1 W.L.R. 991 and in *Littlewoods Mail Order Stores Limited* v. *Inland Revenue Commissioners* [1969] 1 W.L.R. 1241) left the court "with rather sparse guidance as to the principles which should guide the court in determining whether or not the arrangements of a corporate group involve a facade within the meaning of that word as used by the House of Lords in *Woolfson*." His Lordship declined the opportunity to attempt a comprehensive definition of those principles. For a recent exposition of the statutory and judicial processes involved in lifting the veil readers should turn to an article by S. Ottolenghi, "From Peeping Behind the Corporate Veil, to Ignoring it Completely" (53 M.L.R. 338). Those who believe that Cape's actions do not deserve "moral approval" should turn to the Cork Committee's Report where it was suggested that to many "it is unsatisfactory and offensive to ordinary canons of commercial morality that a parent company should allow its wholly-owned subsidiary to fail, or that a company should be permitted by other companies in the same group, and particularly by its ultimate parent, to take commercial advantage from its membership of the group, without there being incurred by those other companies any countervailing obligations" (see *Review Committee on Insolvency Law and Practice* (1982) Cmnd. 8558, para. 1924). As with many of the sentiments expressed by Cork, legislative action is awaited.

DUTIES OF DIRECTORS—ACCOUNTING FOR PROFITS—
QUANTUM MERUIT

Most, if not all, readers will be familiar with Guinness, a dark bodied
stout with a creamy head. Many will also be aware of some of the
events which have embroiled the business of the producer of the
famous drink during the 1980s. Events that have led in 1990 to the
conviction and imprisonment of prominent figures in the world of
business and finance. Less newsworthy but no less significant have
been the attempts to recover the profits that were "creamed off" that
stout body during the period of those same events. The House of
Lords has now given its support to that attempted recoupment, albeit
on different grounds from lower courts. In *GUINNESS PLC* v.
SAUNDERS [1990] 2 W.L.R. 324 W, a director of Guinness, had
provided services to the company in connection with its take-over bid
for Distillers Company plc. In return W, an American attorney had
received via a Jersey-based company £5.2 million from Guinness
upon the successful completion of the take-over. This sum, it was
alleged by W, had been paid in pursuance of an agreement concluded
between himself and a sub-committee of the board of directors of
Guinness. This sub-committee had consisted of the first and second
defendants, namely S and W himself, and a third director. Guinness
sought to recover from W this sum. In reply, W claimed that he was
entitled to the money either because it had been properly authorised
by the sub-committee or because of a *quantum meruit*. Throughout
the proceedings it was assumed that W had acted bona fide.

At first instance Sir Nicholas Browne-Wilkinson had given
judgment against W on the basis that he had received money in
breach of duty as director by reason of his failure to disclose his
interest as required by section 317 of the Companies Act 1985. The
Court of Appeal had rejected W's appeal. However, before the
House of Lords it was accepted that these decisions, founded as they
were upon a breach of section 317, were erroneous. They were
inconsistent with the case of *Hely-Hutchinson* v. *Brayhead Ltd* [1968]
1 Q.B. 549 which had held that failure to comply with the statutory
duty of disclosure rendered any contract voidable at the instance of
the company. On this basis the contract would have had to be
rescinded and W placed in status quo. But this had not been done. In
ordinary circumstances this conclusion might have ended the case
there and then but, according to Lord Goff, there was a simpler
solution based upon Guinness's articles of association. In particular

W's claim that the payment had been properly authorised failed upon the construction of those articles of association, although they were "conspicuous neither for their clarity nor for their consistency (*per* Lord Goff at p. 340). Nevertheless the House concluded that a sub-committee of the board had no power to authorise the remuneration of directors nor could the full board delegate its authority to a sub-committee or any of its members so as to clothe either with any implied actual authority or ostensible authority to agree remuneration. The House also rejected a further argument by W that he was entitled to remuneration under an article which allowed directors to be paid for "professional services." W's services were viewed as being those of a business consultant depolying skills acquired in the exercise of his profession but not as a person acting in a "professional capacity." Thus the purported contract under which W claimed remuneration was void. But W did not rest his claim there.

At the outset Guinness had conceded for the purpose of the action that W had performed valuable services in connection with the bid. Thus it was argued on W's behalf that he was entitled to a sum by way of *quantum meruit* or equitable allowance for his services. In Lord Templeman's opinion the short answer to a *quantum meruit* claim based on an implied contract for reasonable remuneration was that there would be no contract unless entered into by the board pursuant to the articles. W relied upon two cases in support of his claim, *In re Duomatic Ltd.* [1969] 2 Ch. 365 and *Craven-Ellis* v. *Canons Ltd.* [1936] 2 K.B. 403. However, these were distinguished by Lord Templeman, in the former case on the ground that the director's remuneration had been sanctioned or ratified by the shareholders. The case of *Craven-Ellis* was distinguished on the basis that there, the plaintiff had not been a director and thus there had been no conflict between his claim for remuneration and the equitable doctrine which debarred a director from profiting from his fiduciary duty. Nor had there been any obstacle to the implication of a contract between the company and the plaintiff.

Lord Goff preferred to rest his rejection of a *quantum meruit* claim upon the long-established principle that "the directors of a company, like other fiduciaries, must not put themselves in a position where there is a conflict between their personal interests and their duties as fiduciaries, and are for that reason precluded from contracting with the company for their services except in circumstances authorised by the articles of association." In his speech Lord Templeman rehearsed the leading authorities upon which this principle was based, in particular *Aberdeen Railway Co.* v. *Blaikie Brothers* [1854] 1 Macq. H.L. 461, *Barrett* v. *Hartley* [1866] L.R. 2 Eq. 789 and *Bray* v. *Ford*

[1896] A.C. 44. In the first of these Lord Cranworth L.C. had stated that it was a rule of universal application that no one such as a director should be allowed "to enter into engagements in which he had, or could have, a personal interest conflicting, or which possibly might conflict, with the interests of those whom he was bound to protect." Or as Lord Herschell put it in *Bray* v. *Ford*: "It is an inflexible rule of a court of equity that a person in a fiduciary position ... is not, unless otherwise provided, entitled to make a profit; he is not allowed to put himself in a position where his interest and duty conflict." However, even this "inflexible rule" is not without its exceptions. In *Phipps* v. *Boardman* [1964] 1 W.L.R. 993 Wilberforce J. (and subsequently both the Court of Appeal and the House of Lords [1967] 2 A.C. 46) had been prepared to allow that a fiduciary in accounting for profits should be able to claim not only a deduction for necessary expenditure but also an allowance for the skill and labour which had produced the profits. According to Lord Templeman this relaxation was sustainable given the risks incurred in that case by the fiduciaries, who might have made irrecoverable personal losses. Lord Goff also believed that *Phipps* was a decision which could be reconciled with the policy underlying the no-profit rule, in that it did not have "the effect of encouraging trustees in any way to put themselves in a position where their interests conflict[ed] with their duties as trustees." Neither Lord Templeman or Lord Goff believed that the present case warranted any such flexibility from a court of equity, not least when it was open to Guinness, if it though fit, to award W appropriate remuneration. Even so there are other reported decisions in which fiduciaries have been allowed to retain remuneration that has been wrongly earned. In *O'Sullivan* v. *Management Agency and Music Ltd.* [1985] Q.B. 428, for example, a contract between agent and principal was overturned because of undue influence. The agent was required by the Court of Appeal to account for profits but was allowed to retain some part of those profits as a reflection of his contribution to their making. However, a significant difference between the cases of *O'Sullivan* and *Phipps* and the present one is that in the former cases the fiduciary received no monies directly from the trust, whereas in this case W's payment came from Guinness.

W's final claim for relief under section 727 of the Companies Act 1985 was equally easily disposed of by their Lordships. W's claim for relief would have required the court to ignore the fact that the money had been paid under a void contract and received by W as a constructive trustee. For the court to have granted relief would have been a breach of the very principles of equity previously discussed.

AUDITORS—DUTY OF CARE—RIGHTS OF INVESTORS

What standard of care are shareholders entitled to expect from the auditors of a company's accounts? Bloodhounds, auditors may not be (see dicta of Lopes L.J. in *Re Kingston Cotton Mill Co. (No. 2)* [1896] 2 Ch. 279), but how loudly and promptly should the corporate watchdogs bark at the footsteps of approaching loss? How alert should the sleeping guardian be? These questions are particularly pertinent at the time of writing in the aftermath of the collapse of Polly Peck International, which itself followed hard upon the heels of a similar downfall at British and Commonwealth. It would be too simplistic to suggest that neither collapse would have occurred had the respective auditors been more vigilant. Indeed, in the case of Polly Peck there have been traces of egg on more than one face, for in the months immediately preceding its collapse several respected firms of City analysts were advocating the purchase of Polly Peck shares. Nevertheless, questions have been raised about the role played by the auditors in both cases.

The role of auditors has also attracted the attention of the judiciary in recent times, most notably that of the House of Lords in *CAPARO INDUSTRIES PLC* v. *DICKMAN AND OTHERS* [1990] 2 W.L.R. 358. The plaintiff company, Caparo, bought shares in another company, Fidelity plc, at a time when its share price had fallen following the announcement of disappointing results based on the audited accounts. Caparo purchased further shares both before and after Fidelity's annual general meeting at which the audited accounts were presented to shareholders. Eventually Caparo carried out a successful take-over bid for all of Fidelity's shares. The present action arose when it was discovered that Fidelity's accounts were inaccurate and misleading in such a way that an apparent pre-tax profit of £1.3 million should in fact have been shown as a loss of £400,000. Caparo thus commenced an action against (*inter alia*) Fidelity's auditors, claiming that they were negligent in certifying, as they did, that the accounts showed a true and fair view of Fidelity's position. This action was dismissed at the trial of the preliminary issue, namely whether the defendant auditors owed a duty of care to the plaintiffs as investors. However, the latter's appeal was allowed by a majority Court of Appeal (O'Connor L.J. dissenting) which found that, whilst there was no relationship between an auditor and a potential investor sufficiently proximate to give rise to a duty of care at common law, there was such a relationship with individual shareholders, so that an individual shareholder who suffered loss by acting in reliance on negligently prepared accounts, whether by selling or retaining his shares or by purchasing additional shares, was entitled to recover in tort. The House of Lords did not agree.

In the course of their opinions Lords Bridge, Roskill, Oliver and Jauncey considered the wider issue of the general principle underlying the existence and scope of the duty of care which one person may owe to another in the infinitely varied circumstances of human relationships. (This issue is further considered in the Tort section of this volume.) It is hardly surprising, given their Lordships' restrictive approach to this wider principle, that they took the stance they did on the facts of the present case. Thus Lord Bridge concluded that "the auditors of a public company's accounts owe no duty of care to members of the public at large who rely on the accounts in deciding to buy shares in the company." Lord Bridge found support for his view that no such wide duty was owed from the decision of Millet J. in *Al Saudi Banque* v. *Clark Pixley (A Firm)* [1990] 2 W.L.R. 344. In that case, in a judgment reached after *Caparo* had been to the Court of Appeal, Millet J. rejected a claim that a duty of care was owed by auditors to a bank lending to a company on the strength of audited accounts. This was so, regardless of whether the bank was an existing creditor of the company or only a potential creditor. Lord Bridge believed that it would be for Parliament, not the courts, to take the necessary steps to create an unlimited duty. But the relationship established by the Companies Act 1985 between the auditors and the shareholders of a company did not go that far. Lord Bridge equated the interests of shareholders with that of the company, namely to be protected against errors and wrongdoing on the part of corporate management by a properly conducted audit. Negligent failure to perform this duty would be recouped by a claim against the auditor in the name of the company, not by individual shareholders. This approach accords with that taken by the Court of Appeal in *Prudential Assurance Co Ltd.* v. *Newman Industries Ltd. (No. 2)* [1982] Ch. 204 to the effect that the loss in value of members' shares arising from damage to a company caused by alleged management fraud was only a reflection of the company's loss (see M. J. Sterling, "The Theory and Policy of Shareholder Actions in Tort," 50 M.L.R. 468, for a contrary view).

Lord Oliver also stated the primary purpose of the statutory audit of a company's accounts to be to ensure, so far as possible, that the financial information as to the company's affairs prepared by the directors reflected the company's position. This was, first, to protect the company itself from the consequences of undetected errors or wrongdoing and, secondly, to provide shareholders with the information to decide whether to reward or control or remove those appointed to conduct affairs. His Lordship doubted that the legislature, in enacting these provisions for these purposes, could have been inspired also by consideration for the public at large and investors in the market in particular. If it had been necessary to determine the point Lord Oliver could have seen more force in the contention that one purpose of the statutory audit might be to enable a shareholder to exercise his proprietary rights in his shares such as disposing of them. But Lord Bridge could see no distinction between losses which arose either because an existing shareholder sold or retained his shares or because he bought new shares.

Perhaps the decision of the House in *Caparo* should come as no surprise, not least given the tenor of their Lordships recent cases in this area. Firms of auditors across the country have no doubt been drawing a collective breath of relief. Individual shareholders, the numbers of whom have grown as a result of recent pressures to open up the investment market, may feel less sanguine about the degree of protection they can expect either from the judiciary or the legislature (see section 15 of the Companies Act 1989 which substitutes a new section 251 of the Companies Act 1985 so as to provide for regulations to be enacted which will enable listed public companies to send summary financial statements to members who choose them in place of a full report and accounts). Corporate shareholders may have less reason for concern. It is still open for a finding that on the facts of a case a duty is owed by auditors to a take-over bidder whose existence and purpose is known to them (see *J.E.B. Fasteners Ltd.* v. *Marks Bloom & Co (a firm)* [1981] 3 All E.R. 289). As for *Caparo*, there seems to be little room for sympathy. It was a predator which gambled by investing in a falling market. This time the gamble failed, but should it have had the right to protection against failure? Clearly the House of Lords thought not.

CHAPTER 2

CONSTITUTIONAL LAW

JUDICIAL REVIEW—UNFAIRNESS OF HEARING

In *R.* v. *Sussex Justices, ex p. McCarthy* [1924] 1 K.B. 256, Lord Hewart C.J. said at p. 259:

> "a long line of cases shows that it is not merely of some importance, but is of fundamental importance, that justice should not only be done but should manifestly and undoubtedly be seen to be done."

Where, for example, there has been a breach of the rules of natural justice and a person has not been given an adequate opportunity to present his case, it has been possible for the courts to quash any decision by way of certiorari.

A nice problem was presented by the case of *AL-MEHDAWI* v. *SECRETARY OF STATE FOR THE HOME DEPARTMENT* [1989] 3 W.L.R. 1294, where the question was raised as to whether the remedy of certiorari lay to quash the decision of an inferior tribunal where the tribunal in question had acted correctly in the procedure adopted but the applicant had been deprived of the opportunity to put his case to the tribunal, not through any fault of his own, but by the alleged negligence of his own legal advisers.

Al-Mehdawi had been given temporary leave to stay in this country as a student. This leave was extended from time to time but after seven years an application for a further extension was refused and he was finally given notice of the Secretary of State's decision to deport him. He instructed solicitors to appeal against that decision. Because of administrative errors by his solicitors, he was not informed of the date of the hearing and neither he, nor his solicitors, appeared. The adjudicator, who was entitled under the Immigration (Procedure) Rules 1984 to proceed with the hearing if he was satisfied that proper notice had been given, determined the matter on the basis of the documents before him and dismissed the appeal. Mr Al-Mehdawi successfully obtained, by way of judicial review, an order of certiorari to quash the adjudicator's decision. The instant report concerns an appeal to the House of Lords by the Secretary of State against the granting of that order and the refusal of the Court of Appeal to set it aside.

Clearly adjudicators' decisions of this nature are reviewable for procedural impropriety. But must that impropriety be the fault of the tribunal? The respondent clearly felt that it need not. He relied on the case of *R.* v. *Leyland Justices, ex p. Hawthorn* [1979] Q.B. 283 where it was found that the failure of the prosecution to disclose the existence of witnesses had prevented the accused from having a fair trial. The decision was quashed as, according to Lord Widgery C.J., there had been a clear denial of the rules of natural justice. As Taylor J. said in *R.* v. *Diggines, ex p. Rahmani* [1985] Q.B. 1109, and affirmed by [1986] A.C. 475:

" ... it cannot be a proper test as to whether the remedy should be granted, in a case where the aggrieved party is wholly innocent, to ask whether the breach of natural justice has come from the court, the adjudicator, the opposition or from some fault on the part of the applicant's legal advisers."

There is a certain logic in this approach. The court is being asked to review the decision to prevent injustice and the injustice is no less if caused by the failure of the respondent's own legal advisers. It could be argued that a tribunal loses jurisdiction to deal with the matter through the *de facto* absence of a fair hearing rather than through any intention to deprive parties of their basic rights. Yet Lord Bridge of Harwich was clearly concerned about the far-reaching implications of such an approach. For example, in a county court action where a litigant fails to appear at a hearing because his solicitor has neglected to inform him of the date and judgment is given against him in default, one would be loath to introduce considerations of natural justice and open up the possibility of judicial review.

For the Secretary of State it was argued that the rules of natural justice are concerned solely with the propriety of the procedure adopted by the decision maker. The adjudicator had afforded the respondent the opportunity to present his case. He should bear no responsibility for the failure of the respondent's legal advisers, it being totally beyond his knowledge or control. To argue otherwise would open up a Pandora's box. Lord Bridge accepted these arguments, saying that "decision of the Court of Appeal could only be supported at the cost of opening such a wide door which would indeed seriously undermine the principle of finality in decision making." Accordingly the appeal was allowed.

P.A.C.E.—EFFECT OF BREACH OF CODE OF PRACTICE

Over the last year there have been a number of reported cases considering the effect of breaches of the Codes of Practice made under the Police and Criminal Evidence Act 1984. In *R.* v. *WALSH* [1989] Crim.L.R.823 (C.A.), Walsh, who was alleged to have made admissions to police officers in a police cell, appealed against his conviction on the ground that evidence had been obtained in breach of Code C and section 58 of the Act. He claimed that he had requested, but had not been permitted, legal advice; that a contemporaneous record of his interview had not been kept, yet no reason for this had been recorded as required by the Code; and he had not been given the opportunity to read and sign the record of the interview. He denied making any admissions. His appeal against conviction was allowed. The Court found that the evidence should have been excluded. There were clear breaches of section 58 and of Code C. To admit such evidence must have had an adverse effect on the fairness of the proceedings and the judge's conclusion that the breach made no difference could not be supported.

Yet another dispute over alleged admissions occurred in *R.* v. *KEENAN* [1989] 3 All E.R. 598. The appellant was charged with possession of an offensive weapon found in the back of the car he was driving. The police alleged that he had admitted knowing the weapon was there although he denied it was his. The interview was not recorded and the appellant was not given the opportunity to read the note of the interview. This was contrary to the Code of Practice. The trial judge ruled that the evidence was admissible and that any unfairness to the appellant resulting from this breach could be cured by the accused going into the witness box and giving his version of events. Once again the appeal against conviction was allowed. The court said that it could not be assumed that unfairness to the defendant could be cured by his going into the witness box. The evidence has been wrongly admitted.

It is clear that not every breach or combination of breaches of the Code will justify the exclusion of interview evidence. The court, in *Keenan* accepted that breaches must be significant and substantial. It approved Lord Lane in *R.* v. *Delaney* (1989) 88 Cr.App.R. 338 when he said that:

"it is no part of the duty of the court to rule statements inadmissible simply in order to punish the police for failure to observe the codes of practice. But if the breaches are significant and substantial we think it makes good sense to exclude them."

Hodgson J. also makes the point in *Keenan* that an important factor in determining whether to exclude the evidence will be a consideration of the strength of the supporting evidence.

In *R. v. QUINN* [1990] Crim.L.R. 581, the same approach is adopted towards non-compliance with the Code of Practice on the use of identification evidence. Following the arrest of the "Balcombe Street Four," the police found a pistol in their flat which was identified as having been used to shoot a police officer. Suspicion fell on the appellant who at various times had been in custody in the United States and in Éire on terrorist offences. A police officer who had been with the murdered police officer at the time of the shooting went to the Special Criminal Court in Dublin and identified Quinn as the man who had shot his colleague. This identification evidence was subsequently used against the accused when he was put on trial in this country. He appealed against conviction on the ground that the judge erred in admitting the identification evidence. The appeal was dismissed. The accused had refused to stand on an identity parade in relation to the alleged offences in the Irish Republic. The British police had simply to accept whatever arrangements were made by the police in Éire to allow the identification to take place and the courts could not expect English procedural requirements to be complied with by police forces operating abroad. Thus the evidence was not *per se* inadmissible as a result of the breach of the code.

The court stressed that the critical question was the fairness of the criminal proceedings. Lord Lane C.J. said that:

"the function of the judge is to protect the fairness of the proceedings, and normally proceedings are fair if a jury hears all relevant evidence which either side wishes to place before it, but proceedings may become unfair if, for example, one side is allowed to adduce relevant evidence which, for one reason or another, the other side cannot properly challenge or meet, or where there has been an abuse of process, *e.g.* because evidence has been obtained in deliberate breach of procedures laid down in an official code of practice. While a significant and substantial breach of the code may lead to the evidence being excluded even in the absence of bad faith, where the judge is satisfied that there is no unfairness, if necessary by taking account of the circumstances in which the evidence was obtained and bearing in mind the position of the disputed evidence in the case as a whole, he need not exercise his discretion to exclude it."

The appeal was dismissed.

PUBLIC INTEREST IMMUNITY—COURT ORDERS DISCLOSURE

Under the doctrine of public interest immunity the Crown is able to oppose an application for discovery of documents in the course of an action on the ground that disclosure would not be in the public interest. Following *Conway* v. *Rimmer* [1968] A.C. 910, it became clear that such a claim of public interest immunity was not conclusive but that the court would balance two competing factors:

i. The public interest that requires evidence to remain secret, *e.g.* on security grounds or to protect a class of documents, such as high level policy documents;

ii. The interests of justice which must ensure that all relevant evidence is available to the court. The courts have sometimes ordered disclosure against the wishes of the Crown but there is no doubt that there is considerable reluctance to question the minister's judgment, especially in matters relating to national security, unless there is a suggestion of bad faith or error on the part of the minister.

The recent case of *Re HIV HAEMOPHILIAC LITIGATION* (*The Times*, October 2, 1990) provides an example of Crown opposition to disclosure of documents being rejected by the court. The plaintiffs were a group of haemophiliacs or their wives or children, who had become HIV positive as a result of being treated with Factor 8 concentrate, imported from the United States, which was infected with the HIV virus. They brought an action, *inter alia*, against the Department of Health alleging that the Department was in breach of its statutory duty under the National Health Service Act 1977 and was negligent in failing to achieve self sufficiency in blood products for England and Wales. They applied for discovery of some 600 documents relating to the policy of self sufficiency in blood products. The Department of Health opposed discovery, claiming that it would be contrary to the public interest for the documents to be disclosed as they were documents relating to the formulation of policy. It argued that such disclosure would be damaging to the proper functioning of the public service, as secrecy and confidentiality is necessary to ensure a full and frank discussion of the issues involved. It seems that the Department feels that effective, candid advice can only be given to ministers if full confidentiality is ensured.

The Court of Appeal ordered disclosure of the documents, overriding the Department's objections. It accepted that the plaintiffs needed documents revealing the process by which policy decisions were arrived at for the proper presentation of their case. It was necessary for the fair and proper disposal of the case that both sides should know the actual grounds for decisions which led to the continued use of Factor 8 concentrate from the United States. As Bingham L.J. said:

> "The balancing exercise between the public interest immunity and the public interest in a fair trail of the claim made by a large body of grievously injured plaintiffs and in public recognition that the claim had been fairly and openly tried came down decisively in favour of the plaintiffs."

The court did however indicate that certain high level documents prepared for the minister before important meetings need not be disclosed since minutes and other records of what the minister said would be disclosed.

It was decided that the documents should be inspected by the court to decide exactly which documents ought to be disclosed.

PUBLIC ORDER ACT 1986—THREATENING BEHAVIOUR— CONSTRUCTION OF SECTION 4

Section 4(1) of the Public Order Act 1986 states that a person is guilty of an offence if he ...

> "(b) distributes or displays to another person any writing, sign ... which is threatening, abusive or insulting ... with intent to cause that person to believe that immediate unlawful violence will be used against him ... or to provoke the immediate use of unlawful violence by that person or another, or whereby that person is likely to believe that *such violence* will be used or it is likely that *such violence* will be provoked." [Ital added].

In *R.* v. *HORSEFERRY ROAD JUSTICES, EX PARTE SIADATAN* [1990] Crim.L.R. 598, the High Court had to construe the last clause of section 4(1), in particular the phrase "such violence," and determine whether the violence must be an immediate response to the act complained of. The act in question was the distribution of Salman Rushdie's Satanic Verses by Penguin Viking Books Ltd., a novel which had caused great offence to Muslims and, indeed, had led to death threats against the author.

The applicant had sought the issue of a summons against Penguin Viking alleging that the company was in breach of section 4(1) in that it had distributed an abusive and insulting writing whereby it was likely that unlawful violence would be provoked. The magistrate refused to issue a summons, finding that in order to constitute an offence, "such violence" as was referred to in the provision must be "immediate."

The applicant applied for judicial review to have the magistrate's decision quashed by certiorari, alleging that he had misconstrued the statute and had gone outside his jurisdiction. He argued that the use of the word "such" in the phrase "such violence" indicated that the draftsman was referring back to the nearest use of the word "violence" earlier in the section. That occurred in the phrase "immediate use of *unlawful violence*" and was not to be taken as referring to the phrase "*immediate unlawful violence*" two lines previously. The phrase "such violence," he contended, must simply be "unlawful violence" with no requirement of immediacy.

The court adopted a rather more robust approach and considered that the two phrases meant the same. It was held therefore that the words "such violence" referred to the whole of the nearest phrase, which was "immediate use of unlawful violence" and also to the earlier phrase "immediate unlawful violence." Accordingly the concept of immediacy was imported into the phrase "such violence." This, it was considered, was in accord with the whole spirit of section 4 and, indeed, the concept of immediate impact ran through the other public order offences of riot, violent disorder, etc. It would, the court felt, be anomalous if there was a requirement that unlawful violence be "immediate" where there was an intent to produce such a result and not where there was merely a likelihood of it.

The applicant's argument was, therefore, rejected by the court which refused the application.

It is of interest to note the factors used as aids to the interpretation of section 4. First, the court looked at the Law Commission Report on Reform of Public Law Offences which preceded the Public Order Act itself. While the courts are not entitled to look at Hansard as an aid to interpretation (see *Davis* v. *Johnston* [1979] A.C. 264); they are prepared to look at White Papers, Law Commission Reports and other travaux preparatoires. (See *Black Clawson International Ltd.* v. *Papierwerke Waldhof-Aschaffenburg A.G.* [1975] A.C. 591 which is clear authority for consulting official reports to understand the mischief with which the legislation was intended to deal). The clear intention, in drafting the Public Order Act, was to create an offence to deal with an immediate violent response.

The second aid to interpretation was to apply the rule that penal statutes be construed strictly. Where there were two possible meanings, that which limited the scope of the offence was to be preferred.

A further problem of interpretation of section 4 arose in *R.* v. *VA KUN HAU* [1990] Crim.L.R. 518. Here there was an appeal against a conviction under section 4 on the ground that the incident, in which it was alleged that the appellant threatened a bailiff and a police officer with a kitchen cleaver in an excited and aggressive fashion, took place in a dwelling house. While offences under section 4 can be committed both in public or in private, the court confirmed that the wording of section 4(2) excludes dwellinghouses.

POLICE POWERS—CLARIFIED

In *McCONNELL* v. *CHIEF CONSTABLE, MANCHESTER* [1990] 1 W.L.R. 364, the Court of Appeal held that a breach of the peace could take place on private premises. The plaintiff claimed damages for false imprisonment where a police officer arrested him under his common law power of summary arrest to prevent a breach of the peace. The plaintiff had been ejected from a store manager's office by a constable and when he attempted to re-enter the store was arrested. He subsequently appeared before the magistrates but he was not, in fact, bound over to keep the peace.

The essence of the plaintiff's claim was that a police officer had no power to arrest for breach of the peace in the circumstances. It was argued on his behalf that in order for there to be a breach of the peace on private premises it is necessary to find some disturbance which would affect members of the public outside the premises themselves. The court ruled against him at first instance and the plaintiff appealed to the Court of Appeal.

Glidewell L.J., while noting that the point did not appear to have been raised before and that there was no clear authority, could find no warrant for this restriction on the bounds of what constituted a breach of the peace for the purpose of justifying an arrest. These bounds had been clearly stated in *R.* v. *Howell (Errol)* [1982] Q.B. 416, where it was said that an arrest was justified where a breach of the peace was committed: (1) in the presence of the person making the arrest; or (2) where the arrestor reasonably believed that such a breach would be committed in the immediate future by the person arrested although that person had not yet committed any breach; or (3) where a breach had been committed and it was reasonably believed that a renewal of it was threatened.

In addition, it could be inferred from cases, such as *Wilson* v. *Sheock* (1949) J.P. 294 and *Robson* v. *Hallett* [1967] 2 Q.B. 939, that a breach of the peace, sufficient for a binding over, could take place in a private place. Similarly, in *R.* v. *Chief Constable of Devon & Cornwall, ex p. C.E.G.B.* [1982] Q.B. 458, the Court of Appeal seemed to accept that a breach of the peace could take place on private land. The appeal accordingly failed.

In *ABBASSY* v. *COMMISSIONER OF POLICE OF THE METROPOLIS* [1990] 1 W.L.R. 385, the Court of Appeal made some helpful comments on the information which should be given to a suspect on summary arrest. The court approved the guidelines laid down in *Christie* v. *Leachinsky* [1947] A.C. 573 where it was stated that the suspect should be told the true reason for the arrest although technical or precise language need not be used.

Woolf L.J., in the instant case, emphasised that no reference need be made as to the power of arrest whether that power be under common law or statute. He also indicated that whether or not the information given is adequate has to be assessed objectively having regard to the information which is reasonably available to the officer. So, for example, in dealing with a deaf person it would be sufficient if the arresting constable has done what a reasonable person would have done in the circumstances. All in all, he stressed that it was not a technical matter but involves informing the person who is arrested in non-technical and not necessarily precise language of the nature of the offence said to constitute the crime for which he is being arrested. The police frequently have to perform their duties in difficult circumstances when it is unrealistic to expect them to use precise legal language.

PARLIAMENTARY PRIVILEGE

A rare examination of the scope of parliamentary privilege and the relationship between the courts and Parliament on matters of parliamentary privilege occurs in *ROST* v. *EDWARDS* [1990] 2 W.L.R. 1280. Here, an M.P. sued *The Guardian* for libel, following publication of an article which, he alleged, suggested that he was improperly attempting to sell privileged and confidential information which he had obtained as a member of the House of Commons Select Committee on Energy. He wished to call evidence that as a result of the article he had failed to be appointed chairman of that committee, as had been expected, and had been dropped from membership of another committee, the Standing Committee on the Electricity privatisation Bill. The question was whether this evidence related to "proceedings of Parliament" and, as such, fell within the scope of parliamentary privilege.

Article 9 of the Bill of Rights 1688 provides that, "the freedom of speech and debates or proceedings in Parliament ought not to be impeached or questioned in any court or place out of Parliament." This suggests that the courts have no power to consider evidence relating to proceedings in Parliament without Parliament's consent. As Coleridge C.J. said, in *Bradlaugh* v. *Gossett* (1884) 12 Q.B.D. 271, at p. 275, "What is said or done within the walls of Parliament cannot be inquired into in a court of law."

In *Rost's* case the plaintiff tried to distinguish earlier authorities, such as *Dingle* v. *Associated Newspaper Ltd.* [1960] 2 Q.B. 405, where the court held that to impugn the validity of a Select Committee report was contrary to Article 9 of the Bill of Rights. He claimed that the intention in these earlier cases was adversely to question the parliamentary proceedings. He contrasted that with the instant case where, he said, there was no wish to criticise anyone, simply to call as a factual witness a chairman of the Committee of Selection to testify on his deselection from the Standing Committee. There was, he argued, no attempt to ask the court to draw any inference, but there was merely an attempt to lead evidence of fact which could not affect the dignity of the House nor infringe its right of free speech. It was also argued that as extracts from Hansard could now be put before the court without leave of the House, he was entitled to call a witness to further his case.

The court rejected these arguments, saying that they were contrary to the unanimous views expressed in the earlier authorities. Popplewell J. indicated that if the plaintiff wished to call the evidence in question, it was open to him to petition the House. His Lordship accepted that, should Parliament refuse to allow the evidence to be put before the court, the plaintiff might well be severely prejudiced. It was clear that the interests of justice did sometimes clash with Parliament's interest in maintaining its privileges. This, it was said, had led to mighty clashes in the past, as when the Sheriff of Middlesex had attempted to collect the damages awarded against Hansard and was imprisoned by Parliament. Even though the relationship between the courts and Parliament on matters of privilege has never been fully resolved, as Lord Reid said in *Pickin* v. *British Rail Board* [1974] A.C. 765 at 788: "For a century or more both Parliament and the courts have been careful not to act so as to cause conflict between them." Clearly Popplewell J. had no intention of disturbing the comity between courts and Parliament.

The plaintiff also wished to call evidence relating to the Register of Members' Interests. The Solicitor General argued that this should not be permitted as it also fell within the definition of proceedings in parliament and was protected by parliamentary privilege. While considering a number of suggested definitions of the phrase "proceedings in Parliament," the judge concluded that it was clearly impossible to arrive at an exhaustive definition. He was satisfied, however, that the Register fell outside that definition. He concluded: "A line has to be drawn somewhere. As Lord Pearce once said, I do not know, I only feel."

APPLICATION FOR JUDICIAL REVIEW—EFFECT OF DELAY

Section 31(6) of the Supreme Court Act 1981 provides that where there has been undue delay in making an application for judicial review, the court may refuse to grant leave for the making of an application ... if it considers that the granting of the relief sought would be likely to cause substantial hardship to, or substantially prejudice the rights of any person or would be detrimental to good administration. This has to be read in conjunction with Rule 4 of Order 53 of the Rules of the Supreme Court which indicates that an application for judicial review must be brought promptly and in any event within three months from the date when the grounds for the application first arose unless there is good reason for extending the period within which the application is made. On the face of it, these two provisions are not easy to reconcile. However, the relationship between the two provisions was recently considered by the House of Lords in R. v. *DAIRY PRODUCE QUOTA TRIBUNAL FOR ENGLAND AND WALES, EX PARTE CASWELL & ANOTHER* [1990] 2 All E.R. 434.

The applicants wished to challenge the decision of the Dairy Produce tribunal on the ground that it had misconstrued the regulations on which its decision was based. The tribunal decision was given in February 1985. It was not until May 1987 that the applicants became aware of the remedy of judicial review as result of an article which appeared in the Farming Press and then a further five months elapsed before legal aid was granted and the application could be made. Clearly the application had not been brought within the three months specified in Rule 4. But the court had power to extend this period where an application was made late, if it considered there was good reason to do this.

Section 31 then had to be considered. Had there been undue delay? Lord Goff said that the combined effect of the 1981 Act and rule 4(1) was that there was undue delay, for the purposes of section 31(6), whenever the application for leave to apply was not made promptly and in any event within three months from the relevant date. The court might then refuse leave if, in its opinion, the granting of the relief sought would be likely to cause hardship or prejudice or would be detrimental to good administration. The House of Lords agreed with the Court of Appeal and the trial judge that the re-opening of the case after such a lapse of time would be detrimental to good administration. As Lord Diplock pointed out in *O'Reilly* v. *Mackman* [1983] 2 A.C. 237, at p. 280:

> "The public interest in good administration requires that public authorities and third parties should not be kept in suspense as to the legal validity of a decision the authority has reached in purported exercise of decision making powers for any longer period than is absolutely necessary in fairness to the person affected by the decision."

Their Lordships reasoned that, if the applicant's case was successful, many other challenges would be made. Indeed, it was likely that all cases decided by the tribunal back to 1984 would have to be reopened. The evidential problems posed by such a sequence would be immense. The decisions related to the allocation of a finite amount of quota. The practical difficulties in reopening the cases would be enormous. This appeared to their Lordships to be exactly the type of situation which Parliament intended to exclude by the provision in section 31. Accordingly the appeal against the refusal to grant leave to apply for judicial review was dismissed.

Their Lordships did not attempt to define with precision what constituted "good administration." This was because applications for judicial review occurred in many different situations and the need for finality might be greater in one context than in another. What is clear is that it is to be decided independently of questions of hardship or prejudice to the rights of third parties. It is interesting to note that Lord Goff points out that in dealing with an application for leave to apply the judge would be most likely to consider whether there had been undue delay and, if so, to decide whether there was good reason for extending the period under Rule 4. The question of substantial hardship or prejudice and that of the detriment to good administration were, he felt, more likely to the explored in depth at the hearing of the substantive application.

In *R.* v. *SWALE BOROUGH COUNCIL EX PARTE R.S.P.B.* (*The Times*, April 11, 1990), it was held that the court was entitled to refuse relief on judicial review under section 31(6) of the Supreme Court Act 1981 on the grounds of the applicant's undue delay, despite a finding of promptness on the application for leave. This is clearly in line with the approach indicated by Lord Goff in *Caswell*.

CHAPTER 3

CONTRACT

FORMATION OF CONTRACT—TENDERS

One of the first principles of contract law taught to students is that an invitation to tender is not, usually, an offer but is an invitation to treat (see *Spencer* v. *Harding* (1870) L.R. 5 C.P. 561). In *BLACKPOOL AND FYLDE AERO CLUB LTD.* v. *BLACK-POOL BOROUGH COUNCIL* [1990] 1 W.L.R. 1195, a novel question was posed: following an invitation to tender was there a contractual obligation to consider all tenders submitted?

Blackpool BC were the owners of Blackpool Airport and granted concessions for the operation of pleasure flights. The plaintiffs had tendered in the past for the concession with success, and in 1983 were invited to tender for the concession, once again, along with six other parties. The invitation to tender stated "The Council do not bind themselves to accept all or any part of any tender. No tender which is received after the last date and time specified shall be admitted for consideration." The plaintiffs submitted the highest bid, delivered it to the town hall in time, but due to a failure by the town hall staff to empty the letter box the bid was not received in time and in consequence was not considered. Another operator's tender secured the concession.

At first instance it was decided that the defendant's stipulation that tenders received after the deadline *would not* be admitted gave rise to a contractual obligation that tenders received on time *would* be admitted for consideration. On appeal to the Court of Appeal, it was argued that the invitation to tender merely amounted to an invitation to treat and no reading of it could lead to the conclusion that the defendants were undertaking to consider all timely tenders submitted. Bingham L.J., however, decided

"where tenders were solicited from selected parties all of them known to the invitor, and where a local authority's invitation prescribed a clear, orderly and familiar procedure, an invitee was to be protected at least to the extent that if he submitted a conforming tender before the deadline he was entitled, not as a matter of mere expectation but of contractual right, to be sure that his tender would be opened and considered in conjunction with all the other conforming tenders."

In terms of offer and acceptance the analysis of the situation would seem to be as follows: whilst the invitation to tender for the concession was not an offer, implicit in the invitation was an offer to consider the tender, acceptance of which offer was made by compliance with the terms of the tender. The judgment at first instance was therefore upheld and the appeal dismissed.

It is not to be concluded that any call for tenders will necessarily give rise to a contractual obligation to consider a submitted tender. The words of Bingham L.J. would seem to suggest that such a contractual obligation may arise where the invitation to tender is directed to known parties and where the procedure to be followed is clear. An invitation to tender which is general, that is open to anyone, will probably fall outside of the ambit of the Court of Appeal's reasoning.

CONSIDERATION—EXISTING CONTRACTUAL DUTY

For many years the rule from the case of *Stilk* v. *Myrick* (1809) 2 Camp. 317 has loomed large on contract courses. Whilst it has been challenged before the courts and criticised by academic writers, it has remained, in its basic form, untouched since Napoleonic times. However, a recent Court of Appeal decision seems at least to have opened the door to some "refinement" of the rule. The facts of *WILLIAMS* v. *ROFFEY BROS. & NICHOLLS (CONTRACTORS) LTD.* [1990] 2 W.L.R. 1153 concerned carpentry work to be done by the plaintiff, a carpenter, on 27 flats being refurbished by the defendants, a building contractor, for a housing association. The defendants entered into a subcontract with the plaintiff, under which the plaintiff agreed to carry out the carpentry work on the 27 flats for £20,000. It was an implied term of the contract that the defendants would make interim payments to the plaintiff, according to the amount of work done, at reasonable intervals. By April 1986 the plaintiff had completed a large part of the work and had been paid £16,200. At this stage, however, the plaintiff was in financial difficulty as the price of £20,000 was too low to enable him to operate satisfactorily and at a profit.

As the main contract between the defendants and the housing association contained a "penalty clause" for late completion of the work, the defendants were concerned that the carpentry work be finished on time. To this end the defendants promised, on April 9,

1986, to pay the plaintiffs a further sum of £10,300, at a rate of £575 for each flat in which the carpentry work was completed. By the end of May 1986 only one further payment of £1,500 had been made, and the plaintiff, after substantially completing the carpentry work on eight more flats ceased work on the site. The plaintiff then sought to recover the outstanding sums of money promised.

At first instance judgment was given for the plaintiff. On appeal, the defendants sought to argue, first, that the promise to pay an additional £10,300 was unenforceable, because of lack of consideration, and secondly, as the work on the eight flats was not complete, that the defendants were under no obligation to make payment.

The main question for the court was whether there had been consideration given by the plaintiff for the promise by the defendant to pay £575 per completed flat.

In the main judgment, Glidewell L.J. began by noting that the defendants had obtained the following benefits as a result of promising to pay the additional sums: first, the plaintiff continued to work; secondly, no penalty was incurred for delay in completion; and thirdly, the trouble and expense of engaging others to complete the carpentry work was avoided. It was argued on behalf of the defendants that, whilst these practical benefits accrued to the defendants, they did not amount to consideration as there was no benefit in law because the plaintiff was only doing what he was already contractually bound to do. Reliance was placed on *Stilk* v. *Myrick* (1809). Glidewell L.J. reviewed the authorities on this point: *North Ocean Shipping Co. Ltd.* v. *Hyundai Construction Co. Ltd.* [1979] Q.B. 705, *Ward* v. *Byham* [1956] 1 W.L.R. 496, *Williams* v. *Williams* [1957] 1 W.L.R. 148, *Pao On* v. *Lau Yiu Long* [1980] A.C. 614, noting the inter-relationship between the rule in *Stilk* v. *Myrick* and the concept of eonomic duress. His Lordship then explained the present state of the law in the following terms:

> "(i) if A has entered into a contract with B to do work for, or to supply goods or services to, B in return for payment by B; and (ii) at some stage before A has completely performed his obligations under the contract B has reason to doubt whether A will, or will be able to, complete his side of the bargain; and (iii) B thereupon promises A an additional payment in return for A's promise to perform his contractual obligations on time; and (iv) as a result of giving his promise, B obtains in practice a benefit, or obviates a disbenefit; and (v) B's promise is not given as a result of economic duress or fraud on the part of A; and (vi) the benefit to B is capable of being consideration for B's promise, ... the promise will be legally binding."

This statement of the law was said not to contravene the principle in *Stilk* v. *Myrick*, but was a refinement and a limitation of the application of that principle which remained unscathed where, for example, B secured no benefit by the promise. Hence a practical benefit, not merely a legal benefit, sufficed as consideration and the defendant's appeal was dismissed.

Russell L.J., after commenting upon counsels' failure to consider the possible application of the principle of estoppel to the problem raised before the court, said cryptically:

> "Consideration there must still be but, ... the courts nowadays should be more ready to find its existence so as to reflect the intention of the parties to the contract where the bargaining powers are not unequal and where the finding of consideration reflects the true intention of the parties."

In this case the true intention of the parties in their agreement of April 9, apart from reflecting a desire on the part of the defendants to retain the services of the plaintiff, manifested itself as a need to replace a haphazard method of payment by a more formalised scheme involving the payment of a specified sum on the completion of each flat. Even though the plaintiff did not undertake additional work, the terms upon which the work was to be carried out were varied and this, in his Lordship's opinion, was sufficient consideration. This did not constitute any reservation as to the correctness of *Stilk* v. *Myrick*, but was explicable on the following basis: "where ... a party undertakes to make a payment because by doing so it will gain an advantage arising out of the continuing relationship with the promisee the new bargain will not fail for want of consideration." The appeal was dismissed.

Purchas L.J. saw the resolution of the consideration question against the background of the commercial advantage to both sides of the agreement of April 9. Thus the plaintiff would secure payment which would enable him to complete the work and the defendants would secure their position commercially. His Lordship, whilst being aware of the dangers, thought that it was open to the plaintiff to be in deliberate breach of contract so as to "cut his losses" and that a promise not to do so could be consideration. Relying on the words of Lord Hailsham L.C. in *Woodhouse A.C. Israel Cocoa Ltd. S.A.* v. *Nigerian Produce Marketing Co. Ltd.* [1972] A.C. 741, 757–758, Purchas L.J. considered the modern approach to the question of consideration to be that where there were benefits derived by each party to a contract of variation even though one party did not suffer a detriment this would not be fatal to establishing sufficient consideration to support the agreement. On this basis the judge at first instance was entitled to reach the decision that consideration existed. The appeal was dismissed.

The implications of this case for the law of contract could be far-reaching and profound. Far-reaching in the sense that a change in approach to *Stilk* v. *Myrick* must necessitate a change in the rule in *Pinnel's Case* and *Foakes* v. *Beer* and profound in that the concept of consideration may have changed. Certainly the latter appears to be the view of Russell L.J. who said

> "whilst consideration remains a fundamental requirement before a contract not under seal can be enforced, the policy of the law in its search to do justice between the parties has developed considerably since the early 19th century when *Stilk* v. *Myrick* was decided ... In the late twentieth century I do not believe that the rigid approach to the concept of consideration to be found in *Stilk* v. *Myrick* is either necessary or desirable."

His Lordship then stated that the courts should be ready to reflect the intention of the parties to the contract by finding consideration. The judgments may be seen as signalling a series of developments.

First, their Lordships each acknowledged the inter-relationship between consideration, where there is a pre-existing contractual duty, and the doctrine of economic duress. The rule in *Stilk* v. *Myrick* has been explained by Treitel as a method whereby the courts could protect the promisor from blackmail, but he doubted whether, in the light of the development of the doctrine of economic duress, the rule continued to serve any useful purpose (see Treitel *The Law of Contract* (7th ed.), pp. 74–76). Whilst the Court of Appeal did not refer to the above view, its words would seem to have this effect.

Secondly, the Court of Appeal has taken the principle in *Stilk* v. *Myrick*, a fairly straightforward and simple rule, and shrouded it in a great deal of uncertainty. The three judgments display a variety of approaches to the main question of the existence of consideration. Whilst, perhaps in Russell L.J.'s judgment, consideration is discernible in the form of something promised so as to vary the existing promise, namely a different payment system and a different system of working, additional consideration is difficult to find in the other judgments. The "practical benefits" obtained by the defendant would have been secured in any event had the plaintiff performed his original contractual obligations. It is therefore difficult to see how these benefits differ from what was originally promised. Is not the instant case decided on the same basis as *Watkins* v. *Carrig* 21 A. 2d. (1941), even though Purchas L.J. declined to follow the American case? Was this not a situation where a promise was obtained, without duress, as a result of a commercially reasonable renegotiation and on that basis it should be enforced? Of course such an approach would mean that *Stilk* v. *Myrick* was no longer law, but perhaps this would represent commercial reality and promote certainty in this area of the law.

Thirdly, the *Roffey* case, while addressing an important issue in the law concerning consideration, does not offer a clear rule or approach to the issue. For example, Russell L.J. stated that

> "the courts nowadays should be more ready to find its existence so as to reflect the intention of the parties to the contract where the bargaining powers are not unequal and where the finding of consideration reflects the true intention of the parties."

This may allow the courts to do "justice," but the problems of application of such an approach are considerable. Presumably such an approach would only apply to a variation of an existing contract and not to the formation of a contract.

Fourthly, the Court of Appeal raised the possibility of dealing with the consideration problem by use of the doctrine of estoppel. Glidewell L.J. referred to an argument raised in the case, that it may be possible for a person, who has been promised an additional payment for services which he is in any event bound to render under an existing contract or by operation of law and on which the promisee has relied, to show that the promisor is estopped from claiming that there was no consideration for his promise. However, as this point had not been argued at first instance, and only mentioned in outline before the Court of Appeal, their Lordships did not offer an opinion on this point.

Finally, as to the question whether only substantial completion of the work on the flats entitled the plaintiff to payment, all three judges, in reliance on the principle in *Hoenig* v. *Isaacs* [1952] 2 All E.R. 176, refused to interfere with the finding of the judge at first instance that there had been substantial completion of the work due under the contract. It is at least arguable that the Court of Appeal has extended the law by allowing sums to be awarded where work has not been wholly completed. *Hoenig* v. *Isaacs* has been considered to support the proposition, that if the *quantity of work* has been completed, but it is defective in part as to *quality*, then the court may make a finding of substantial performance. In the instant case, the Court of Appeal was prepared to allow a finding of substantial completion, even though on the facts as found the work on none of the flats had been completed.

Readers may be interested to read some of the commentaries which have been published since *Roffey* was decided: Adams and Brownsword, "Contract, Consideration and the Critical Path" (1990)

53 M.L.R. 536; Halson, "Sailors, Sub-Contractors and Consideration" (1990) 106 L.Q.R. 183; and Birks, "The Travails of Duress"
[1990] L.M.C.L.Q. 342.

MISREPRESENTATION—ONUS OF PROOF—ASSESSMENT OF
DAMAGES

For a representation to give rise to the remedies consequent upon a
misrepresentation, there must not only be a false statement of fact,
but also reliance on that statement, which induces the formation of a
contract. Under the requirement of inducement, *inter alia*, two
conditions must be satisfied. First, the misrepresentation must be
material, which means that the statement should be such as to affect
the judgment of a reasonable man. This is obviously an objective
test. Secondly, the representation must be relied upon by the
representee. This depends upon the representee's actual state of mind
and therefore is subjective. The question of where the burden of
proof lies in relation to inducement was considered in *MUSEPRIME
PROPERTIES LTD.* v. *ADHILL PROPERTIES LTD.* (*The Times*,
March 13, 1990).

In this case the plaintiff entered into a contract to buy property
from the defendant by reason of inaccurate statements both by the
auctioneer and in the auction particulars. The statements were to the
effect that rent from leases, to which the property was subject, was
negotiable. Counsel for the defendant argued, *inter alia*, that even
though the plaintiff had been misled, the misrepresentation had not
been material, because no reasonable bidder would have allowed that
to affect his bid. Scott J. rejected this argument, and cited with
approval the following passage from Goff and Jones, *The Law of
Restitution* (3rd ed. 1986) p. 168):

> "In our view any misrepresentation which induces a person to enter into a contract
> should be a ground for rescission of that contract. If the misrepresentation would
> have induced a reasonable person to enter into the contract, then the court will . . .
> presume that the representee was so induced, and the onus will be on the
> representor to show that the representee did not rely on the representation either
> wholly or in part. If, however, the misrepresentation would not have induced a
> reasonable person to contract, the onus will be on the misrepresentatee to show
> that the misrepresentation induced him to act as he did. But these considerations
> go to the question of the onus of proof. To disguise them under the cloak of
> 'materiality' is misleading and unnecessary."

In consequence, as the misrepresentation would have induced a
reasonable person to make the contract into which the plaintiff

entered, the onus of proof fell on the defendant. The burden was not discharged and therefore the plaintiff was entitled to rescind the contract. The court also awarded damages for the conveyancing costs the plaintiff had uselessly incurred.

It is to be noted that the view expressed by Goff and Jones, that the requirement of materiality is to be doubted, is not one shared by Treitel. In Treitel, *The Law of Contract* (7th ed.), p. 260, he argues in view of the wide definition afforded to "materiality" and the existence of the exception—that in cases of fraudulent misrepresentation the perpetrator will not be allowed to argue that the representation was immaterial—the requirement of materiality is not unreasonable. He concludes:

> "An immaterial representation would necessarily relate to a matter of trivial importance so that its falsity would cause no substantial loss to the representee. If the representor has made such a representation in good faith it is hard to see why a representee should be entitled to any relief when, by definition, the representation would not have influenced a reasonable man."

Certainly, materiality and the distinction to be drawn between it and reliance is one which has been recognised in the case law on this point. For example, in *Smith* v. *Land and House Property Corporation* (1884) 28 Ch.D. 7 at 16, Bowen L.J. said:

> "I cannot quite agree ... that if a material representation calculated to induce a person to enter into a contract is made to him it is an inference of law that he was induced by the representation to enter into it ... "

The clear implication is that both materiality and reliance are required for there to be an actionable misrepresentation.

A second case, *NAUGHTON AND ANOTHER* v. *O'CALLAGHAN* (*The Times*, February 17, 1990), raised the issue of the measure of damages for misrepresentation. In this case the plaintiff bought a colt, on the strength of its stated pedigree, for £27,300, with a view to training and racing it. The horse was raced in 1982 and 1983 without much success. It was discovered in mid-1983 that the horse did not have the pedigree described. The plaintiffs issued a writ in 1985 claiming breach of contract and misrepresentation.

The main issue reported concerned the measure of damages to be awarded under section 2(1) of the Misrepresentation Act 1967. Waller J. made it plain that the principle to be applied was that relating to an action in tort and that the award of damages was to put the plaintiffs in the position they would have been in had the representation not been made to them. Evidence established that if the horse had been correctly described it would have fetched £23,500. However, after it had been raced unsuccessfully and the misdescription had been discovered, the value had fallen to £1,500. As the relief claimed by the plaintiffs was damages, not rescission, the question arose as to the time at which the value of the retained horse was to be assessed. Was it to be the value as at the time of purchase or at the time of discovery of the misrepresentation? Obviously the ultimate value of the horse, that is £1,500, was as a result of it having been raced unsuccessfully.

Waller J., in answer to this problem, commenced by citing the rule stated in *McGregor on Damages* (15th ed) that in relation to shares: "The normal measure of damages is the purchase price of the shares less the actual value if any at the time of acquisition." After noting that this was a rule of general application, he considered the following words of Winn L.J. in *Doyle* v. *Olby* [1969] 2 Q.B. 158:

" ... where [there is] a fraudulent inducement, the proper starting point for any court called upon to consider what damages are recoverable by the defrauded person is to compare his position before the representation was made to him with his position after it, [brought about by that misrepresentation] always bearing in mind that no element in the consequential position can be regarded as attributable loss and damage if it be too remote a consequence."

Whilst *Doyle's* case related to fraud, Waller J. said that a claim under the Misrepresentation Act, was to be approached in the same way. Further support for the court having a discretion as to the date for assessment of damages was drawn, by analogy, from a breach of contract case, *Johnson* v. *Agnew* [1980] A.C. 367. In that case Lord Wilberforce indicated that, whilst damages will normally be assessed as at the date of the breach, this is not an absolute rule and if it would give rise to injustice, the court has power to fix such other date as may be appropriate in the circumstances.

The instant case, said Waller J., was distinguishable from the situation in which the normal rule for the timing of the assessment of damages applied for the following reasons: first, what the plaintiffs in fact purchased in reliance on the misrepresentation was a different animal completely; secondly, if they had known of the misrepresentation within a day or so they could and would have sold the horse for its then value; thirdly, their decision to keep the horse and race it was precisely what the sellers would have expected; fourthly, the fall in the value of the horse if it did not win races was not due to a general fall in the market for racehorses but was special to this horse. In consequence the plaintiffs were allowed to recover the difference between £27,300 and £1,500.

The plaintiffs were also awarded damages for consequential losses. In this case, the losses arose from the upkeep and training of the horse. As the plaintiffs had expended money on the horse in reliance on the representation made, which they would otherwise not have spent, they were entitled to a sum which would put them in the position they would have been in had the misrepresentation not been made.

It is interesting to note that his Lordship was also prepared to award the same damages had there been, alternatively, a breach of contract. It should be noted that the rules of remoteness for fraudulent and negligent misrepresentation differ, as the rule under the former allows recovery of damages for *all* consequential losses (see Lord Denning's judgment in *Doyle* v. *Olby*), whereas under the latter, the losses must be reasonably foreseeable. In this case the consequential losses had to be and were, reasonably foreseeable as the plaintiff's claim was for negligent misrepresentation.

SALE BY DESCRIPTION—MERCHANTABLE QUALITY

The first question faced by the Court of Appeal in *HARLINGDON AND LEINSTER ENTERPRISES LTD.* v. *CHRISTOPHER HULL FINE ART LTD.* [1990] 3 W.L.R. 13 was whether, on a sale of a painting by one art dealer to another, there was a "sale by description" within section 13 of the Sale of Goods Act 1979. Unfortunately, there is no statutory definition of the phrase in question and, as Slade L.J. remarked, the guidance to be derived from the cases is 'surprisingly limited."

The facts of the instant case were clear; however, the inferences to be drawn from them as a matter of law were less certain. The seller had telephoned the buyer and said that he was in a position to sell two paintings by Gabriele Munter. He reasonably believed that the paintings were by Munter, although such attribution was outside his area of expertise. An employee of the buyer visited the seller's gallery for the purpose of deciding whether to buy the pictures and of that occasion the judge, at first instance, said:

> "Hull [the seller] did say that he did not know much about the paintings. He said that he had never heard of Gabriele Munter and thought little of her paintings. He made it absolutely plain that he was not an expert. By some form of words which no one can now precisely remember Hull to a certain extent made it clear that he was relying on Runkel [the buyer's employee]."

Subsequently, after the buyer had purchased and, in turn, resold one of the paintings it was positively identified as a forgery.

The buyer claimed that the seller was in breach of the implied condition in section 13(1) of the Sale of Goods Act 1979 which provides: "Where there is a contract for the sale of goods by description, there is an implied condition that the goods will correspond with the description." In short, he claimed that the seller had undertaken a contractual obligation that the painting was a Munter as described. Crucial to this argument was the question of whether there was a contract for the sale of goods "by description" and on this point the judges of the Court of Appeal disagreed.

Nourse L.J. agreed with the judge at first instance who had said:

> "In my judgment such a statement [as to the artist] could amount to a description and a sale in reliance on it could amount to a sale by description within the meaning of the Act. However, on the facts of this case, I am satisfied that the description by Hull before the agreement was not relied on by Runkel in making his offer to purchase which was accepted by Hull. I conclude that he bought the painting as it was. In these circumstances there was not in my judgment a sale by description."

Thus, on this view of the facts, the crucial issue was as to reliance or non-reliance on a descriptive statement. The statement could be discounted where the buyer could be said to be buying the "specific thing" rather than a "specific thing corresponding to a description."

By contrast, Stuart-Smith L.J. (dissenting) argued that had Runkel visited Hull after the telephone conversation and bargained about the price and then bought, there could have been no doubt that there was a sale by description. How then, he reasoned, could it come about that what was otherwise a sale by description should cease to be one? This, on the facts, could only arise as a result of what passed between Hull and Runkel. If Hull had said that he did not know one way or the other whether the painting was genuine (despite his description) and that Runkel must make up his mind for himself on this point, then this could well have rendered the earlier descriptive statement inoperative. However, it was his Lordship's view that Hull's statement, that he knew nothing of Munter and that he did not like her paintings, was neutral as to the impact of the earlier descriptive statement which remained operative. Nor did the fact that Hull recognised that the buyer was more expert in the field of Munter's work cancel or withdraw what had been said previously. His Lordship concluded that:

> "It would be a serious defect in the law if the effect of a condition implied by statute could be excluded by the vendor's saying that he was not an expert in what was being sold or that the purchaser was more expert than the vendor. That is not

the law; it has long been held that conditions implied by statute can only be excluded by clear words. There is nothing of that kind in this case. ... I can find no evidence that justified the judge in finding that Mr. Runkel made up his own mind and relied on his own judgment to the effect that the painting was genuine. And it seems to me to be quite contrary to his evidence."

The third judge in the Court of Appeal, Slade L.J., gave a careful explanation of the meaning to be attributed to the phrase "sale by description":

"the fact that a description has been attributed to the goods, either during the course of negotiations or even in the contract (if written) itself, does not necessarily and by itself render the contract one for 'sale by description.' If the court is to hold that a contract is one 'for the sale of goods by description,' it must be able to impute to the parties (quite apart from section 13(1) of the Sale of Goods Act 1979) a common intention that it shall be a term of the contract that the goods will correspond with description. If such an intention cannot be imputed to the parties, it cannot be said that the contract is one for the sale of goods by description within the ordinary meaning of the words. The practical effect of section 13(1) ... is to make it plain ... that in a case where such a common intention *can* be imputed, the relevant term of the contract will be a condition as opposed to a mere warranty."

Following this explanation Slade L.J. examined the proposition, relied upon by the judge at first instance and adopted by Nourse L.J. (above), that there must be actual reliance on a description if there is to be a "sale *by* description." He concluded that this was not strictly correct as, on principle, although proof of reliance was essential if a party to a contract wished to claim relief in respect of a misrepresentation as to a matter which did not constitute a term of the contract, relief in respect of a breach of a term in a contract could be claimed irrespective of reliance. Put simply, relief in respect of a breach of contract turns upon whether there is a term and whether it is broken. However, whether there is a term depends upon the intention of the parties (actual or presumed) and in this matter the presence or absence of reliance may be significant in so far as it casts light on the intention of the parties. As Slade L.J. indicates in relation to the facts of the instant case:

"If there was no ... reliance by the purchaser, this may be powerful evidence that the parties did not contemplate that the authenticity of the description should constitute a term of the contract—in other words, that they contemplated that the purchaser would be buying the goods as they were."

Slade L.J. could see no sufficient grounds for disturbing the inference of the judge at first instance and concluded that there had been no sale by description.

The second question faced by the Court of Appeal was as to whether the forged painting was of merchantable quality within section 14(2) of the Sale of Goods Act 1979. Section 14(6) provides that:

> "goods of any kind are of merchantable quality ... if they are as fit for the purpose or purposes for which goods of that kind are commonly bought as it is reasonable to expect having regard to any description applied to them, the price (if relevant) and all the other relevant circumstances."

At first instance Judge Oddie found that the purpose or purposes for which goods of this kind (the picture) are commonly bought is aesthetic enjoyment. This finding was attacked on appeal on the ground that a sale between one dealer and another has the purpose of resale. Nourse L.J., whilst accepting the criticism of the original finding, nevertheless concluded that even if the purpose was both resale and aesthetic enjoyment, this painting (sold for £6,000), although a forgery, was still capable of resale (albeit for only £50–£100) and of providing aesthetic enjoyment. The fact that the painting could only be sold at a loss could not, on this view, render the painting not reasonably fit for resale. Moreover, even if a description which had not been relied upon could still be treated as a description "applied to goods," because of the non-reliance this was regarded as insignificant, as was the issue of price where the buyer had determined the figure on his own assessment of the value of the picture. Slade L.J. did not embark upon any detailed analysis of merchantability, being content to say that if the only complaint was as to the identity of the artist and, as he found, there was no term that Munter was the artist then there was no room to "succeed through the back door of section 14."

Stuart-Smith L.J., consistent with his view that the buyer should succeed under section 13, would also have allowed the appeal on the ground that the picture was unmerchantable under section 14(2). Judge Oddie had found, without citing authority, that merchantable quality did not relate to anything other than the "physical quality of the goods sold." The judge considered that the goods in question undoubtedly constituted a picture and that it was fit for use as such. Stuart-Smith L.J. categorically rejected this approach, holding that it is not correct to confine the question of quality to physical matters but further, that the question of whether something is a fake or genuine is a quality of the goods themselves. Whilst he accepted that a sale of a specific picture consisting simply of oil on board, without any description as to the identity of the artist, would be merchantable provided it was fit for display and aesthetic enjoyment, he did not consider this applicable to the circumstances of the instant case. He reasoned that if, because of absence of reliance, there was technically no sale by description then nevertheless the court was required to consider the matters listed in section 14(6) (above). These included the description of the painting as being by Munter and the price. Moreover, both parties were aware that the purpose was not merely putting the picture on the wall but was essentially resale. He concluded that, having taken these factors into account, it would defeat the reasonable expectation of the buyer if a virtually worthless fake was found to be fit for the purpose of being sold as a painting by Munter at a price of around £6,000. His Lordship was reinforced in his finding by the view of Mustill L.J., in *Rogers* v. *Parish (Scarborough) Ltd.* [1987] Q.B. 933 at 944, where in speaking of the sale of a Range Rover for £14,000, it was said that: "The buyer was entitled to value for his money."

Where does this case leave the law on sale or, perhaps more pertinently, where does it leave the law on the sale of pictures between dealers? It appears that the majority approach should be characterised as dictated by a policy directed towards supporting the operation of the market. Nourse L.J., in commenting on evidence which had been adduced as to the usage or custom of the London art market, accepted that many dealers habitually deal with one another on the basis of *caveat emptor*. He concluded that:

> " ... the astuteness of lawyers ought to be directed towards facilitating, rather than impeding, the efficient working of the market. The court should be exceedingly wary in giving a seller's attribution any contractual effect. To put it in lawyer's language, the potential arguability of almost any attribution, being part of the common experience of the contracting parties, is part of the factual background against which the effect, if any, of an attribution must be judged."

By way of contrast, Stuart-Smith L.J., whilst emphasising that he was not influenced by the fact that this was a "hard case," concluded that should the buyers fail " ... it is undoubtedly a hardship on the [buyers], who have refunded the price to their purchaser, [and] are left holding the loss, when the [sellers] ... would appear to have a claim over against those who sold the painting to them."

It may be that the judgment of Stuart-Smith L.J. reflects a technically correct application of law which is less influenced by external policy considerations than those of his brethren. Indeed, the judgment of Slade L.J. may be perceived as leading almost inexorably to the conclusion reached in the dissenting judgment until the crucial point at which it was necessary to either accept or reject the inferences to be drawn from the evidence and findings of primary fact. Although Slade L.J. chose to defer to the findings of the judge at first instance nevertheless his judgment presents a classically succinct lesson on the law of sale.

MEASURE OF DAMAGES

The case of *SEALACE SHIPPING CO. LTD.* v. *SHIPPING LTD.* (*The Times*, September 25, 1990) raised the question of what was an appropriate measure of damages where, in breach of contract, a seller failed to deliver part of the goods sold. In this case the contract was for the sale of a ship, together with a spare propeller. The sellers in breach of contract failed to supply the propeller. Ultimately, the main issue was as to the measure of damages recoverable for the failure to supply the propeller. This question was posed before an arbitrator, who decided that if the propeller had been delivered it would have had a scrap value of US $1,100, and this sum was recoverable by way of damages. On appeal to the High Court, Steyn J. held that the arbitrator had erred in ignoring the buyers' interest in having the propeller for potential use if the occasion arose and the appropriate measure of damages was the reasonable cost of replacing the spare propeller. This cost was assessed at US $121,000. The sellers appealed to the Court of Appeal.

Neill L.J., in considering the problem raised, noted the following: first, where there was a breach of contract the injured party was to be put, as far as money is able to do so, in the position he would have been in had the contract been performed; secondly, this principle was, however, qualified by another principle, namely that the plaintiff must take all reasonable steps to mitigate the loss consequent on the breach; thirdly, the duty to mitigate was not contractual in nature, and was as described by Pearson L.J. in *Darbishire* v. *Warran* [1963] 1 W.L.R. 1067, at p. 1075, in the following words:

> "the plaintiff is not entitled to charge the defendant by way of damages with any greater sum than that which he reasonably needs to expend for the purpose of making good the loss. In short, he is fully entitled to be as extravagant as he pleases but not at the expense of the defendant."

In the light of the approach to the assessment of damages in *Radford* v. *De Froberville* [1977] 1 W.L.R. 1262 (see below), his Lordship posed the question: what damage had the buyers really suffered as a result of the non-delivery of the propeller?

In the opinion of Neill L.J., the arbitrator had not erred in *law* and had taken into account the interest of the buyer in having the spare propeller for potential use if the occasion had arisen. However, the arbitrator, in considering whether the buyers were likely to or needed to obtain a replacement for the missing spare propeller, had decided on the *facts* that in the particular circumstances of the case the commercial value of *that* spare propeller on *that* ship was no more than its scrap value. Accordingly the decision of the arbitrator was restored and the appeal of the sellers allowed.

The problem raised by this case was essentially as to the basis of assessment to be employed to put the buyer in the position he would have been in had the contract been performed. The two possibilities were, the "difference in value" (*i.e.* between what was paid for and what was delivered) or the "cost of cure" (*i.e.* providing a replacement for the missing propeller). Under the Sale of Goods Act 1979, section 51 states that the measure of damages, where there is an available market, is prima facie to be ascertained by the difference between the contract price and the market price. However, in this case, due to the lack of a market in such propellers, the above rule could not be applied. Hence the court fell back on the general rule of what loss naturally flowed from the breach. It was noted by Steyn J., in the High Court, that no authority was cited in the sale of goods context for the proposition that the buyers must prove a genuine intention to replace missing goods in order for the cost of cure standard to apply. The Court of Appeal by implication held that *Radford* v. *De Froberville* did establish such a rule, and that it should apply to sales of goods. On the facts there was no evidence to suggest that the buyers intended to buy a replacement propeller, therefore a difference in value measure was the correct standard to apply *i.e.* the propeller's scrap value.

FRUSTRATION—WHETHER SELF-INDUCED—FAULT

Frustration of contract is an area fraught with conceptual and practical difficulties. This is particularly true of the relationship between frustration and fault, and the application of the concept of self-induced frustration. The case of *J. LAURITZEN A.S.* v. *WIJSMULLER B.V. (The "Super Servant Two")* [1990] 1 Lloyd's L.R. 1, provided the Court of Appeal with an opportunity to consider the application of the doctrine. Lauritzen (L) owned a large drilling rig which was under construction in a Japanese shipyard. L contracted in writing with Wijsmuller (W), who were specialised carriers by sea, for the carriage of the rig from Japan to the Rotterdam area of the North Sea. By the contract, the rig was to be transported by " ... Super Servant One or Super Servant Two in

Wijsmuller's option." The rig was to be delivered to W between June 1981 and August 1981 and the price was payable in two instalments, half at the commencement of carriage and half upon delivery.

On January 29, 1981, several months before the rig was to be tendered for carriage, Super Servant Two foundered and was a total loss; this, alleged W, was the vessel they intended to use to transport L's rig. Super Servant One, had been scheduled to carry and did carry, cargo under two other contracts over the expected period of the performance of the contract with L. L alleged that the Super Servant Two was lost due to W's negligence, which was denied by W. As the case concerned certain preliminary issues and the facts had not been investigated, the court proceeded to consider the alternative situations in turn.

On February 16, 1981, W informed L that they could not fulfill their contractual obligations and a further agreement was reached in April, under which the rig would be transported by a different method between July and October. This alternative method of transport caused loss and increased expense to the parties and was the immediate cause of the present litigation.

L alleged that W was in breach of contract, while W pleaded that the contract was frustrated. At first instance, Hobhouse J. decided, *inter alia*, that the contract had not been frustrated.

Before considering the application of the doctrine of frustration to the facts, Bingham L.J. in the Court of Appeal helpfully summarised the relevant law. The starting point was the statement of the modern law by Lord Radcliffe in *Davis Contractors Ltd.* v. *Fareham UDC* [1956] A.C. 696 at p. 729:

> " ... frustration occurs whenever the law recognises that without default of either party a contractual obligation has become incapable of being performed because the circumstances in which performance is called for would render it a thing radically different from that which was undertaken by the contract ... It was not this that I promised to do."

From the case law certain propositions were established beyond question:

1. The doctrine of frustration evolved to mitigate the rigour of the common law's insistence on literal performance of absolute promises. The purpose was to achieve a just and reasonable result, in a situation where enforcement of the literal terms of a contract, after a significant change in circumstances, would be unjust (*Hirji Mulji* v. *Cheong Yue Steamship Co. Ltd.* [1926] A.C. 497).

2. Since the effect of the doctrine is to kill the contract and discharge the parties from further liability under it, the doctrine is not

to be lightly invoked, must be kept within narrow limits and ought not to be extended (*Pioneer Shipping Ltd.* v. *B.T.P. Tioxide Ltd. (The Nema)* [1982] A.C. 724).

3. Frustration brings the contract to an end forthwith, without more and automatically (*Hirji Mulji*, above).

4. The essence of frustration is that it should not be due to the act or election of the party seeking to rely on it (*Hirji Mulji*). A frustrating event must be some outside event or extraneous change of situation (*Paal Wilson & Co. A/S* v. *Partentreederi Hannah Blumenthal (The Hannah Blumenthal)* [1983] 1 A.C. 854).

5. A frustrating event must take place without blame or fault on the side of the party seeking to rely on it (*The Hannah Blumenthal*).

His Lordship first considered if the contract was frustrated where the loss of the Super Servant Two occurred without the negligence of the defendants. The problem was that the contract provided for the transport to be effected by either the Super Servant One or Two, therefore the loss of one did not make the performance of the contract something radically different. Bingham L.J. decided that as the contract did provide for an alternative, it was not frustrated. Moreover, as the defendants had argued that the contract was frustrated on February 16, 1981, upon their communication to L that they would not perform the contract, this, thought his Lordship, was inconsistent with the contract coming to an end automatically. Another difficulty in the defendant's argument was that it was irreconcilable with *Maritime National Fish Ltd.* v. *Ocean Trawlers Ltd.* [1935] A.C. 524. In that case the interposition of human choice after the alleged frustrating event was regarded as fatal to the plea of frustration.

The second question to be considered was as follows: what is meant by saying that a frustrating event, to be relied on, must occur without the fault or default, or without blame attaching to, the party relying on it? It was argued on behalf of the defendants that application of the doctrine of frustration was only precluded where that party had acted deliberately or in breach of an actionable duty in causing the frustrating event. In this case neither condition existed as, first, it was not alleged that W deliberately sank the vessel, and, secondly, no duty of care to L was owed by W (indeed, on this latter point the court had held that no such duty was owed). The defendant thus argued that it was doubtful whether mere negligence would render an event self-induced and therefore preclude frustration. The plaintiffs argued for a less restrictive approach. Reliance was placed on the words of Griffiths L.J. in *The Hannah Blumenthal* [1983] 1 A.C. 854 at p. 882:

"The essence of frustration is that it is caused by some unforeseen supervening event over which the parties to the contract have no control and for which they are not therefore responsible. To say that the supervening event occurs without the default or blame or responsibility of the parties is, in the context of the doctrine of frustration, but another way of saying it is a supervening event over which they had no control. The doctrine has no application and cannot be invoked by a contracting party when the frustrating event was at all times within his control ..."

This was accepted by the Court of Appeal. The argument put forward on behalf of W was considered to be too restrictive and did not address the real question, which was whether the frustrating event relied upon was truly an outside event or extraneous change of situation, or whether it was an event which the party seeking to rely on it had the means and opportunity to prevent, but nevertheless caused or permitted to come about. In this case, if the Super Servant Two had been lost due to the negligence of W, their servants or agents, then frustration was precluded.

The appeal was dismissed. Dillon L.J. considered an argument expressed by Treitel in *The Law of Contract* (7th ed.) at pp. 674–675 and 700–701. In Treitel's view, where a party has entered into a number of contracts with other parties and an uncontemplated supervening event results in him being unable to perform all those contracts, he can, provided he acts "reasonably" in making his election, elect to use such means as remain available to him to perform some of the contracts, and claim that the others, which he does not perform, have been frustrated by the supervening event. This view, in his Lordship's opinion, was inconsistent with the view expressed by Lord Wright in *Maritime National Fish*, where he said at p. 529:

" ... the case could be properly decided on the simple conclusion that it was the act and election of the appellants which prevented the St Cuthbert being licensed for fishing with an otter trawl. It is clear that the appellants were free to select any three of the five trawlers they were operating and could, had they willed, have selected the St Cuthbert as one, in which event a licence would have been granted to her. *It is immaterial to speculate why they preferred to put forward for licences the three trawlers which they actually selected.* (italics added) Nor is it material, as between the appellants and the respondents, that the appellants were operating other trawlers to three of which they gave the preference."

Also the view of Treitel was inconsistent with the rule that a frustrating event brought the contract to an end immediately.

The Super Servant Two is a welcome decision on a difficult area of law. Several points raised in this case are worthy of note. First, an example of the restrictive approach of the doctrine has been provided. Bingham L.J. indicated that if the contract had only

provided for carriage by the Super Servant Two (instead of specifying
the alternative of the Super Servant One), then assuming no
negligence by W, the contract would have been frustrated. This
illustrates the essence of frustration, which is to consider what was
contractually agreed between the parties and whether the supervening
event has radically altered the nature of the obligation. Clearly on the
facts of this case, no such alteration had taken place, the contract
could be performed by the Super Servant One.

Secondly, it is necessary to identify the event that *causes* the
contractual obligation to become radically different. In the instant
case the root cause of the alleged frustrating event was not the
sinking of the vessel but the election by W not to use the Super
Servant One to perform the contract with L. As this was not an
extraneous event, it fell within the rule in *Maritime National Fish*
concerning self-induced supervening events.

Thirdly, had the issue of causation not been fatal to W's claim
then, in any event, negligence on the part of W in the sinking of the
vessel would have precluded a successful plea of frustration. Bingham
L.J. considered that a frustrating event had to be an event which
arose 'without blame or fault on the side of the party seeking to rely
on it," and that in the circumstances a "fine legal test was
inappropriate; what was needed was a pragmatic judgment whether a
party seeking to rely on an event as discharging him from a
contractual promise was himself responsible for the occurrence of that
event." Whilst his Lordship, in this passage, adopts a robust
approach towards the issue of fault, it ought to be noted that not
every degree of fault will disable a party from claiming frustration.
As Lord Russell indicated in *Joseph Constantine Steamship Line Ltd.*
v. *Imperial Smelting Corporation Ltd.* [1942] A.C. 154 at p. 179:

> "The possible varieties [of fault] are infinite and can range from the criminality of
> the scuttler who opens the sea-cocks and sinks his ship, to the thoughtlessness of
> the prima donna who sits in a draught and loses her voice. I wish to guard against
> the supposition that every destruction of corpus for which a contractor can be said,
> to some extent or in some sense, to be responsible, necessarily involves that the
> resultant frustration is self-induced within the meaning of the phrase."

Finally, whilst this is undoubtedly an important case, in a precedent
sense it does not carry the same weight as a Court of Appeal
decision. This is because it was decided by a two-person court on an
interlocutory appeal. Therefore, as students of the English legal
system know, a later Court of Appeal is not, following the exception
created in *Boys* v. *Chaplin* [1968] 2 Q.B. 1, bound by such a case.
However, it is to be remembered that a later court will not depart

from a previous decision unless there is some valid reason for doing so.

CHAPTER 4

CRIMINAL LAW

ATTEMPT—PROBLEM OF PROXIMITY

In *R.* v. *JONES* [1990] 1 W.L.R. 1057, the Court of Appeal was called upon to rule as to the proper construction of section 1(1) of the Criminal Attempts Act 1981, which provides:

> "If, with intent to commit an offence to which this section applies, a person does an act which is more than merely preparatory to the commission of the offence, he is guilty of attempting to commit the offence."

Section 4(3) provides that:

> "Where in proceedings against a person for an offence under section 1 above, there is evidence sufficient in law to support a finding that he did an act falling within subsection (1) of that section, the question whether or not his act fell within that subsection is a question of fact."

The defendant, who had pointed a sawn-off shotgun, with the safety catch in the "on position," at his ex-mistress' new lover, was charged with, *inter alia*, attempted murder. Defence counsel submitted that the charges should be withdrawn from the jury, there being insufficient evidence of attempted murder since the defendant would have had to perform at least three more acts before the full offence could have been completed. Those acts were: (1) to remove the shotgun's safety catch; (2) to put his finger on the trigger; and (3) to pull it. The trial judge rejected this submission and the defendant was convicted. He appealed against conviction to the Court of Appeal on the ground that the trial judge erred in law in his construction of section 1(1) and ought to have withdrawn the case from the jury.

Defence counsel now submitted that for about a century two different tests as to the *actus reus* of attempt had been inconsistently applied by the courts. First, there was the so-called "last act test" derived from *R.* v. *Eagleton* [1855] Dears 515, according to which the accused would be guilty of an attempt if he had done the last act he expected to do and which it was necessary for him to do in order to achieve the consequence alleged to be attempted. That had been referred to by Lord Diplock in *D.P.P* v. *Stonehouse* [1978] A.C. 55

in the graphic phrase: "In other words the offender must have crossed the Rubicon and burnt his boats," (p. 68). Secondly, there was the test derived from *Stephen's Digest of the Criminal Law* (9th ed., 1950) Chap. IV article 29 where it was stated: "An attempt to commit a crime is an act done with intent to commit that crime and forming part of a series of acts which would constitute its actual commission if it were not interrupted," (pp. 24–25). Defence counsel argued that section 1(1) of the 1981 Act (above) had not resolved the question as to which was the appropriate test and submitted that it was the *Eagleton* test which should be adopted.

Taylor L.J., reading the judgment of the Court of Appeal, observed that defence counsel's submission amounted to an invitation to construe the words of the statute by reference to previous conflicting case law. In the court's opinion, that was misconceived. The 1981 Act was a codifying statute which amended and set out completely the law relating to attempts and in those circumstances " ... the correct approach is to look first at the natural meaning of the statutory words, not to turn back to the earlier case law and seek to fit some previous test to the words of the section," (p. 1061). That approach, it was noted, had been adopted by the Court of Appeal in *R.* v. *Gullefer* (Note) (1990) 1 W.L.R. 1063, where Lord Lane C.J. had stated that:

> "The first task of the court is to apply the words of the Act of 1981 to the facts of the case. Was the appellant still in the stage of preparation to commit the substantive offence, or was there a basis of fact which would entitle the jury to say that he had embarked on the theft itself? ... we do not think that it is necessary to examine the authorities which preceded the Act of 1981 ... ,"

(p. 1065). His Lordship had then added, referring to the two lines of authority mentioned above: "It seems to us that the words of the Act of 1981 seek to steer a midway course. They do not provide ... that the *R.* v. *Eagleton* test is to be followed ... ," (p. 1066). In his view, the Act's words gave perhaps as clear a guidance as possible in the circumstances as to the time at which an attempt began: "It begins when the merely preparatory acts have come to an end and the defendant embarks upon the crime proper," (p. 1066). The Court of Appeal in the present case stated that it adopted those words and rejected defence counsel's contention that section 1(1) of the 1981 Act in effect embodied the "last act" test derived from *Eagleton*.

The question for the judge in the present case, then, Taylor L.J. added, was whether there was evidence from which a reasonable jury properly directed could conclude that the defendant had done acts which were more than merely preparatory. The defendant's actions in obtaining, shortening and loading the gun, donning his disguise and making his way to the venue for the planned ambush could only be regarded as preparatory acts. But, in the court's view, once he had pointed the loaded gun at the victim with the intention of killing him, there was, in his Lordship's opinion, sufficient evidence for the consideration of the jury on the attempted murder charge. It was a matter for them to decide whether they were sure those acts were more than merely preparatory. In the court's opinion, therefore, the trial judge was right to allow the case to go to the jury and the appeal against conviction was, accordingly dismissed.

As with the terms of section 1(1) of the 1981 Act itself, the ruling in the present case does nothing to alleviate the basic difficulty of identifying what conduct is and what is not an attempt but, nevertheless, the present ruling is welcome. Earlier decisions of the Court of Appeal under the 1981 Act left unclear the precise relevance to the statutory offence of attempt of the various tests propounded at common law on the issue in question. In *R.* v. *Widdowson* (1985) 82 Cr.App.R. 314 and *R.* v. *Boyle and Boyle* (1987) 84 Cr.App.R. 270, the court felt itself entitled to look back to and apply common law tests in reaching its decision on attempt, whereas, as noted above, in *Gullefer* the court repudiated the so-called "Rubicon" test referred to in the present case and declared that the words of the 1981 Act gave the clearest guidance on the issue. The forceful support in the present case for the *Gullefer* approach to the matter has now clarified the law in this area.

THEFT—APPROPRIATION

The conflict between the decisions of the House of Lords in *R.* v. *Lawrence* [1972] A.C. 626 and *R.* v. *Morris* [1984] A.C. 320 as to the nature of "appropriation" for the purposes of theft, contrary to section 1 of the Theft Act 1968, (*Lawrence* asserting that an act can amount to an appropriation of property even though it is done with the property owner's consent; *Morris* declaring that appropriation must involve an unauthorised act) formed the background for the controversial decision in the civil case of *DOBSON* v. *GENERAL ACCIDENT FIRE AND LIFE ASSURANCE CORPORATION PLC* [1989] 3 W.L.R. 1066, where the Court of Appeal (Civil Division) was strongly critical of *Morris* and supportive of *Lawrence*.

The plaintiff had a home insurance policy with the defendant company covering him against "loss or damage caused by theft." He advertised a watch and a diamond ring for sale for £5,950 and agreed the sale over the phone with a man who responded to the advertisement. It was agreed that payment would be by a building society cheque in favour of the plaintiff. Next day, the plaintiff handed over the goods in return for the cheque. After paying the cheque into his bank, he was informed that the cheque had been stolen and was worthless. The plaintiff claimed on his insurance policy to recover the value of the watch and ring but the defendant company denied liability on the ground that the circumstances of the loss did not amount to theft within the meaning of section 1(1) of the Theft Act 1968 which provides: "A person is guilty of theft if he dishonestly appropriates property belonging to another with the intention of permanently depriving the other of it; ... " Section 3 of the Act provides: "(1) Any assumption by a person of the rights of an owner amounts to an appropriation ... " The plaintiff sued to recover the value of the goods in the county court where the recorder held that his loss was caused by theft and gave judgment for the plaintiff. The defendant appealed to the Court of Appeal on the grounds, *inter alia*, that: (1) the recorder had erred in finding (a) that the plaintiff had suffered loss caused by theft within the terms of the insurance policy and (b) that there had been an appropriation of the plaintiff's watch and ring; and (2) the recorder had misdirected himself in finding that there had been a usurpation of the plaintiff's rights having previously found that the thief had acquired a voidable title to the goods.

In the Court of Appeal Parker L.J. noted that in *R.* v. *Lawrence* (above) the House of Lords had stated that the words "without the consent of the owner" were not to be placed after 'appropriates" in section 1(1) (above) so that "appropriation" could occur even though the owner had consented to the property being taken. Having referred to the four constituent elements of theft His Lordship said that on the basis of *Lawrence* the facts of the present case appeared to establish that the rogue assumed all the rights of an owner when he took or received the goods from the plaintiff. That he did so dishonestly and with the required intention was beyond doubt. However, he added, it was submitted, relying upon sections 17 and 18 of the Sale of Goods Act 1979, that the fourth element of theft was missing because, at the time of appropriation, the goods were not property "belonging to another." The property had, it was submitted, already passed to the rogue at the time the articles were delivered to him. It had passed either: (a) at the time of the agreement of sale which was, arguably, concluded over the phone, or (b) at a later time, when the agreement of sale was concluded just prior to the rogue receiving the goods in exchange for the cheque. Parker L.J. rejected this submission. Having regard to the terms of the contract, the conduct of the parties and the circumstances of the case, he had no doubt that the property was not intended to pass in this case on contract but only in exchange for a valid building society cheque. Parker L.J. was supported in this view by Bingham L.J. His Lordship added that, following both *Lawrence* and *Morris*, even if it could be regarded as intended to pass in exchange for a false, but believed genuine, cheque, it would not avail the defendant.

It was further submitted by the defendant that, notwithstanding the statement of the House of Lords in *Lawrence* that absence of consent on the owner's part was not an ingredient of theft and was not relevant to the question whether there had been an appropriation, the later decision of the House in *Morris*, (above) that appropriation "involves not an act expressly or impliedly authorised by the owner but an act by way of adverse interference with or usurpation of those rights," (p. 332), must lead to the conclusion that in the present case there had been no theft. Parker L.J. referred to several points of difficulty he considered to be presented by the decision in *Morris* but concluded that:

> " ... whatever *R. v. Morris* did decide it cannot be regarded as having overruled the very plain decision in *R. v. Lawrence* ... that appropriation can occur even if the owner consents and that *R. v. Morris* itself makes it plain that it is no defence to say that the property passed under a voidable contract,"

(p. 1075).

Despite his emphatic support for the *Lawrence* approach to the issue of appropriation and consent, Parker L.J. went on to approve two decisions widely thought to be consistent with the *Morris* approach, namely, *R. v. Skipp* (1975) Crim.L.R. 114 and *R. v. Fritschy* (1985) Crim.L.R. 745, on the basis that in these cases "there was much more than mere consent of the owner. There was express authority ... " (p. 1075). This was felt to be a basis on which these cases could be reconciled with both *Lawrence* and *Morris*.

Returning to the present case, Parker L.J.'s conclusion was that the defendant's contention that there was no theft was negatived, in so far as it was based on consent, by *Lawrence*, and, in so far as it was based on the fact that the contract was voidable and not void, by *Morris* which ruled this fact to be irrelevant. Therefore, while recognising that in so doing he might be said not to be applying *Morris*, His Lordship concluded by stating that if consent and the existence of a voidable contract under which property passes were irrelevant, there was, in his view, a plain interference with or usurpation of the plaintiff's rights. The appeal was, accordingly, dismissed.

Despite the criticism of it in the present case, the House of Lords' decision in *Morris* remains the leading authority on the matter in question and, although it may well have been open to criticism in a number of respects, in its central recognition of appropriation as involving an unauthorised act or conduct to which the owner does not consent, it seems to reflect more appropriately than does the ruling in the present case the essential quality of the "assumption" of the rights of the owner referred to in section 3(1) of the 1968 Act. According to the *Oxford English Dictionary*, to "assume" is to "lay claim to" and this suggests that what is required, in theft, is conduct on the accused's part indicating to others that the property is his to do as he likes with—" ... something in the way of an assertion of dominion over the property," (Professor E. Griew, *The Theft Acts 1968 and 1978* (6th ed.), para. 2–79)—rather than conduct consented to by the owner which implicitly recognises and respects the owner's rights. As Professor J.C. Smith states: "A person does not 'assume' the rights of an owner if the owner has conferred those rights on him," (*The Law of Theft* (6th ed.), para. 31). It is the *Morris* approach, considered by Professor Smith to be correct in principle, which accords with the intention of the Criminal Law Revision Committee, upon whose report the 1968 Act was largely based (see *Eighth Report, Theft and Related Offences*, Cmnd. 2977, para. 35).

The present ruling throws the law concerning the nature of appropriation in theft into confusion and uncertainty. This is a particularly unfortunate development in relation to an offence which has to be dealt with so frequently by judges and juries. What, for example, are they to make of a situation where to suffice as an act of appropriation an act need not be done without the owner's consent but must be done without his authority? This decision seems to bear out Professor Griew's earlier opinion that: " ... the cases ... have repeatedly suggested that rationalisation and consistency do not have high priority as judicial objectives in this context," (*The Theft Acts 1968 and 1978*, (5th ed.), para. 2–47).

RECKLESSNESS—RECENT DEVELOPMENTS

Recent years have seen an unfortunate advance of the extended concept of recklessness propounded by the House of Lords in *R. v. Caldwell* [1981] 2 W.L.R. 509. It has extended beyond its origins in the statutory offences of criminal damage (*Caldwell*, above), reckless driving and causing death by reckless driving (*R. v. Lawrence* [1981] 2 W.L.R. 524), into the common law of manslaughter (*R. v. Seymour* [1983] 2 All E.R. 1058; *R. v. Goodfellow* (1986) 83 Cr.App.R. 23).

However, two recent decisions of the Court of Appeal have confirmed that *"Caldwell* recklessness" is to have no application to those non-fatal offences against the person contained in the Offences Against the Person Act 1861.

In the first case, *R. v. MORRISON* (1989) 89 Cr.App.R. 17, the Court of Appeal confirmed that *"Caldwell* recklessness" is to have no application in relation to the offence of unlawfully and maliciously wounding or causing grievous bodily harm with intent contrary to section 18 of the Offences Against the Person Act 1861 which provides:

> "Whosoever shall unlawfully and maliciously by any means whatsoever, wound or cause any grievous bodily harm to any person ... with intent to resist ... the lawful apprehension or detainer of any person shall be liable ... to [imprisonment] ... "

Several police officers entered a vacant property to evict squatters and make arrests for burglary. The defendant hid behind a door in an upstairs room. A woman police officer entered the room saying, "We are police officers, you are under arrest," whereupon the defendant dashed towards the window. The woman police officer seized him by the clothes, but he dived forward through the glass of the window, dragging her with him as far as the window where her face was severely lacerated by the broken glass. The defendant was charged with wounding with intent to resist arrest contrary to section 18 (above). He was convicted after the trial judge had initially directed the jury on recklessness as follows:

> "Recklessness presupposes something in the circumstances that would draw the attention of an ordinary, prudent and sober person to the possibility that the act that he is committing is capable of causing harm to her (in other words, the woman), and that that risk that he was then going to take was more than just a possibility: it was a risk which he either took deliberately, or he closed his mind to the possibility of causing her injury."

Later, after exchanges on the matter between counsel and the trial judge in which it was suggested that in fact the appropriate test of recklessness was not the objective one put to the jury by the judge but, rather, was the subjective test, the trial judge told the jury as they were about to retire that " ... it is whether this defendant—not whether the ordinary, prudent and sober person would appreciate the risk involved ... " The defendant appealed against conviction to the Court of Appeal on the ground, *inter alia*, that the trial judge had misdirected the jury on the question of recklessness in relation to an offence against section 18 (above).

Lord Lane, delivering the judgment of the Court of Appeal, explained the nature of the two types of recklessness currently applied in different areas of the criminal law.

First, *"Caldwell* recklessness"—this had been propounded, in the context of the Criminal Damage Act 1971, in *R.* v. *Caldwell* [1981] 2 W.L.R. 509 by Lord Diplock who said:

> "In my opinion, a person charged with an offence under section 1(1) of the Criminal Damage Act 1971 is reckless as to whether any such property would be destroyed or damaged if (1) he does an act which in fact creates an obvious risk that property will be destroyed or damaged and (2) when he does the act he either has not given any thought to the possibility of there being such risk or has recognised that there was some risk involved and has nonetheless gone on to do it," (p. 516).

This was the objective test, Lord Lane explained, involving not what the defendant himself was thinking but what an ordinary, reasonable and prudent observer would in those circumstances have thought.

Secondly, *"Cunningham* recklessness"—defined by Byrne J. in *R.* v. *Cunningham* [1957] 2 Q.B. 396, where the Court of Criminal Appeal, having considered various cases under the 1861 Act, approved of the classic statement made by Professor Kenny that:

> "In any statutory definition of a crime, malice must be taken not in the old vague sense of wickedness in general but as requiring either (1) an actual intention to do the particular kind of harm that in fact was done; or (2) recklessness as to whether such harm should occur or not (*i.e.* the accused has foreseen that a particular kind of harm might be done and yet has gone on to take the risk of it."

(*Outlines of Criminal Law* (1st ed., 1902)). The decision in *Cunningham*, Lord Lane stated, still stood and was still binding on the Court of Appeal since, although Lord Diplock considered and distinguished it in *Caldwell*, he did not in fact disapprove of it. The principle stated in *Cunningham*, Lord Lane added, was repeated by Mr. Turner in his 10th edition of *Russell on Crime* where it was stated, *inter alia*, that "We think that this is an accurate statement of the law ... In our opinion the word 'maliciously' in a statutory crime postulates foresight of consequences" (at p. 1592). In the present case, his Lordship observed, the word "maliciously" appeared in the section under consideration and in the indictment. Consequently, it was that definition of "recklessness" which applied here.

In the court's view, the trial judge's second direction on recklessness was insufficient to alert the jury to the fact that they were considering *Cunningham* rather than *Caldwell*. Any revision of his earlier direction on recklessness should have been more detailed, emphasizing to the jury that the matter for their consideration was what was going on in this man's mind, and not in the ordinary prudent observer's mind. If the jury had had it brought home to them that it was the subjective test which they had to apply, they might have come to a different conclusion as to the guilt or innocence of the defendant, the court concluded, and, therefore, the appeal had to be allowed and the conviction quashed.

In the second case, *R.* v. *SPRATT* [1990] 1 W.L.R. 1073, the Court of Appeal has similarly confirmed that the test of recklessness to be applied in the context of the offence of assault occasioning actual bodily harm, created by section 47 of the Offences Against the Person Act 1861, is *"Cunningham* recklessness."

The Defendant fired an air pistol from his flat and two of the pellets hit a young girl playing outside. He claimed that he had not realised that there were people there at the time he fired the pistol. The defendant pleaded guilty to, *inter alia*, one count of assault occasioning actual bodily harm, contrary to section 47 (above). He pleaded guilty to that count on the basis that he was reckless in that he failed to give thought to the possibility of a risk that he might cause actual bodily harm. By accepting his plea on that basis, the trial judge by implication ruled that it did amount in law to the offence charged. On his appeal against sentence, the Court of Appeal suggested that the hearing be adjourned so that a submission could be made that that ruling was wrong in law. The defendant contended, *inter alia*, that: (1) whilst he accepted that there was an obvious risk that if he fired the air weapon out of the window it might cause injury; (2) he did not think of that at the time and did not realise that there were people present at the time; (3) he was incorrectly advised by counsel that his instructions disclosed no defence in law, in that he was advised that on his instructions he was reckless; and (4) he was incorrectly advised that the appropriate test of recklessness was that propounded in *Caldwell*, (above), whereas the correct law was the test of recklessness propounded in *Cunningham*, (above).

Counsel for the prosecution submitted that the trial judge's decision to accept the plea on the basis tendered was not wrong in law because it fell within the definition of recklessness formulated in *Caldwell* (above) and it was that concept of recklessness which was applicable to a charge of assault occasioning actual bodily harm.

Defence counsel submitted, however, that *"Caldwell* recklessness" had no application to such a charge. The appropriate test of recklessness in this context was *"Cunningham* recklessness." The leading modern authority supporting this contention is *R.* v. *Venna* [1976] Q.B. 421 where the Court of Appeal confirmed that intention or recklessness as to the relevant consequence resulting from one's conduct would suffice as *mens rea* in assault offences. *Venna* was approved by the House of Lords, by Lord Elwyn-Jones L.C. in *D.P.P.* v. *Majewski* [1977] A.C. 493 and by Lord Diplock in *Caldwell* as authority for the proposition that recklessness was enough to constitute the necessary *mens rea* in assault cases. In *Venna*, the notion of recklessness seen as relevant to assault offences was "*Cunningham* recklessness," knowledge of risk being required on the accused's part.

Counsel for the prosecution, however, argued that that no longer applied to cases under section 47 of the 1861 Act, although it still applied under section 20 (unlawfully and maliciously wounding or inflicting grievous bodily harm) and section 23 (unlawfully and maliciously administering a noxious thing) of that Act due to the presence of the term "maliciously" therein. Counsel relied upon *R.* v. *Seymour* [1983] 2 All E.R. 1058 where Lord Roskill had stated: "*Reckless* should today be given the same meaning [*i.e.* the *Caldwell* meaning] in relation to all offences which involve 'recklessness' as one of the elements unless Parliament has otherwise ordained" (p. 1064).

McCowan L.J., delivering the judgment of the Court of Appeal, stated that the words "unless Parliament has otherwise ordained" might well have been intended to refer not only to modern Acts of Parliament which used the term "recklessly" but also to the 1861 Act where the word "maliciously" was used. However, he explained,

> " ... the history of the interpretation of the Act of 1861 shows that, whether or not the word 'maliciously' appears in the section in question, the courts have consistently held that the *mens rea* of every type of offence against the person covered both actual intent and recklessness, in the sense of taking the risk of harm ensuing with foresight that it might happen. Hence, according to judicial interpretation of the Act of 1861, these are all instances where Parliament 'has otherwise ordained' " (p. 1082).

In the Court of Appeal's view, Lord Roskill's statement in *Seymour* (above) appeared to be *obiter* and, in any event, the court could not believe that by the use of those words the House in *Seymour* had intended to cast any doubt upon the decisions in *Cunningham* or *Venna*. The Court of Appeal considered itself bound by the decision in *Venna*, and it followed that the basis upon which the defendant pleaded guilty did not amount to an offence in law. Therefore, the defendant's conviction had to be quashed.

The Court of Appeal's declaration in the present case of the position regarding section 47 is all the more significant in that the earlier decision of the Divisional Court in *D.P.P.* v. *K (a minor)*

[1990] 1 All E.R. 331, had appeared to proceed on the assumption that "*Caldwell* recklessness" was to be applied thereto. The Court of Appeal in the present case declared that *D.P.P.* v. *K* was wrongly decided.

The two cases reported above will undoubtedly reinforce the opinion of those readers who share the regret expressed by Lord Lane in *Morrison* that: "Unhappily there are now in the law of this country two types of recklessness according to the nature of the crime which is charged" (p. 19). Few areas of the criminal law can be in greater need of reform.

FALSE ACCOUNTING BY OMISSION

The offence of false accounting is defined in section 17 of the Theft Act 1968, which provides:

> "(1) Where a person dishonestly, with a view to gain for himself or another or with intent to cause loss to another,—(a) destroys, defaces, conceals or falsifies any account or any record or document made or required for any accounting purpose; ... he shall, on conviction on indictment, be liable to imprisonment for a term not exceeding seven years. (2) For purposes of this section a person who ... omits ... a material particular from an account or other document, is to be treated as falsifying the account or document."

In an extraordinary ruling in *R.* v. *SHAMA* [1990] 1 W.L.R. 661, the Court of Appeal, in order to bring an unusual case of pure omission within the scope of section 17, has, in effect, re-written the phrase "made or required" therein to mean "made or required or *required to be made*."

The defendant was employed by British Telecommunications Plc as an international telephone operator. As part of his duties he was required to record details of each call to an overseas subscriber on one of a number of identical printed forms (known as a charge ticket) which were later used for accounting purposes. He connected certain subscribers without filling in a charge ticket and was charged with four counts of false accounting contrary to section 17(1)(*a*) of the Theft Act 1968 (above) in that by failing to complete the appropriate charge tickets he thereby omitted material particulars from a document required for an accounting purpose. He was convicted and appealed against conviction to the Court of Appeal on the ground, *inter alia*, that the trial judge had erred in law by wrongly deciding that the evidence disclosed false accounting under section 17. Whilst not disputing that a completed charge ticket would be a "record or document made or required for any accounting purpose," defence counsel argued that the section could only apply to an identifiable document and, here, there was no such document, no charge ticket having been completed in respect of any of the four relevant calls. Therefore, it was submitted, the facts disclosed no offence under section 17.

Pill J., reading the judgment of the court, observed that if the defendant's argument was correct some curious results would follow. First, if the operator dishonestly omitted one or more material particulars, he committed an offence, but if he omitted all material particulars (which the court felt was, in practice, the only way in which the fraudulent system could be operated), he committed no offence. Secondly if, instead of being supplied with a pile of tickets, one to be used for each call, the operator was given a sheet (or several sheets) on which the necessary details had to be filled in seriatim, covering each one of a series of calls, the omission of one complete line of details on a sheet would amount to an offence, because the sheet in question would be an identifiable document. This example, the court felt, highlighted the artificiality of the defendant's argument. Pill J. explained that as soon as a local subscriber contacted the operator and asked to be connected to a foreign subscriber, it was the operator's duty to fill in the requisite details on one of the standard form tickets in the pile in front of him. It would not matter which ticket he filled in. Each of the words in section 17 had to be given a meaning if possible, Pill J. added, noting that the legislature had used the phrase "made or required ... " in paragraph (a). The court's opinion was that:

> " ... as soon as the operator's duty arose, one of the standard printed forms became a document 'required' for an accounting purpose. The document is the standard form provided for the operator at his place of work which he should fill in as part of his work and which is required for accounting purposes," (p. 665).

In the court's view, the fact that the operator may have had more than one of the forms in front of him at the material time did not prevent there being an identifiable document for the purposes of section 17. A supply of forms for each call was to be expected and the fact that the operator might choose to pick up one rather than another of the identical forms did not mean that no document was in existence. The court concluded, therefore, that the prosecution were not obliged to do what, by definition, they could not do, namely to produce a charge ticket relevant to the call referred to in each count. They had only to satisfy the jury that the defendant had dishonestly and, for the purpose specified in the opening words of section 17, failed to complete a charge ticket by omitting material particulars from a document required for an accounting purpose. The appeal was, accordingly, dismissed.

What is particularly regrettable about the straining of the language of section 17 to cater for conduct such as that in the present case is that such fraudulent practices would appear to fall quite readily within the ambit of the deception offence created by section 2 of the Theft Act 1978 which covers, *inter alia*, dishonestly securing the remission of a debt, or dishonestly inducing the creditor to forgo payment of a debt.

CHAPTER 5

ENGLISH LEGAL SYSTEM

CURRENT TRENDS

At a time when more emphasis was placed on the teaching of legal history as part of first year courses on the English Legal System, it was possible to illustrate and explain the development of our legal institutions by references to certain enduring themes. Two such were the opposing tendencies towards (a) uniformity and centralisation and (b) the requirements of justice for the continued availability of local courts. The latter has always seemed the slightly weaker of the two, although the reform of the County Courts in the mid-nineteenth century is a prime example of an intention to look after local needs, whilst the replacement of the Assize system following the Beeching Report of 1969 was more of a balancing act between the needs of strong central guidance and the availability of local courts for the administration of justice.

The 20 years since Beeching and the Courts Act of 1971 have seen the evolution of new themes. So, whilst the old themes continue to be relevant in assessing the shape of present reforms, they have been joined by two others. The Courts and Legal Services Act 1990 is only the centre piece through which the themes continue to be developed. The *COURTS AND LEGAL SERVICES ACT 1990*, was reviewed at its Bill stage in the 1990 Nutshell. The Bill survived largely unscathed during its passage through Parliament. The two new themes are, first that the legal system must provide "value for money" and secondly, the principle now enshrined in the statutory objective set out in Part II of the 1990 Act, that there should be new ways (*i.e.* a variety of ways involving competition with established procedures and institutions) of developing legal services, particularly advocacy, litigation, conveyancing and probate services.

As with the old or traditional themes referred to at the outset, one of the new themes will be the dominant one, although both are concerned with worthwhile objectives; some critics have already indicated that "value for money" simply means cheaper and, by implication, inferior services. It is too early to judge, and the writer believes that some of the proposals noted below should be assessed on their merits as to whether they promote a better administration of justice or not, rather than being simply cost cutting and time saving devices.

Such themes may provide the basis for a critical analysis of recent changes and proposals for change which may appear as the subject-matter of examination questions and assignments. Although some of the changes are tentative in nature, they merit consideration as an indication of the way the legal system may change over the medium to long term. The remainder of this brief review of current trends within the English Legal System will be devoted to some illustrative material. For convenience of reference in revising, these examples are divided between civil and criminal justice with a preliminary note on the professions. It must be stressed that these are examples only and are by no means a complete list of the relevant developments and changes. In some cases, it may be argued that the final effect of combining new ways of delivering "legal" services with "value for money" may be to de-legalise the activity altogether. Consider, for example, the combined effect of new technology and business techniques and the new arrangements permitted under the Courts and Legal Services Act 1990 on the provision of conveyancing services.

The Legal Profession

The Courts and Legal Services Act 1990 enables changes to be made to the structure of the legal professions but it also preserves the self-regulatory powers of the Bar and the Law Society. However, the following additional points should be noted. In due course solicitors and other professionals may acquire extended advocacy rights. Already, designated members of staff of the Crown Prosecution Service, who are not legally qualified, may appear in court in connection with bail applications. The Bar has introduced new arrangements for training, including the payment of salaries to pupils and is encouraging the adoption of new management schemes for Chambers, designed to improve the chances of survival for an independent Bar. The European Directive on Mutual Recognition of Qualifications, which comes into force early in 1991, must have a long-term effect on the professions as it may result in it being easier for a French "avocat" to become an English solicitor than for an English barrister to become a solicitor.

Civil Justice

The work of the Court of Appeal remains central to the administration of justice in civil matters. In his report for 1989–90, the Master of the Rolls recorded that approximately only one-quarter of appeals were successful. He went on to stress the need for advisers to give proper advice to potential appellants; pointing out that disappointment with a judicial decision was not a sound reason for an appeal. The Courts and Legal Services Act 1990 would, he indicated, empower the Rule Committee to extend the classes of case in which leave to appeal was required. After a pilot study last year, the judges of the Court of Appeal were confident that hopeless appeals could be identified as a very early stage. The report also indicated that the Court now had a team of in-house lawyers which, with the aid of an improved computer system, would be able to bring about improvements in the management of cases in the Court of Appeal. Attention was drawn to the weekly list of cases where those concerned should show cause whereby the case should not be dismissed for failure to comply with the rules. The biggest cause of cases appearing in that list was a failure to lodge with the court an approved note of the reasons for the judgment under appeal. The profession was warned that it should improve and that the rules would be rigorously enforced. Fifty-three appeals had gone forward to the House of Lords, and in only one-third of them had the House reversed or varied the decision of the Court of Appeal. The principal proposal, illustrative of the themes referred to above, which affects the civil courts, is a suggestion that certain classes of dispute (*e.g.* building disputes and some personal injury cases) should be resolved without a court hearing at all. This would be done by adopting the American system of "alternative dispute resolution" (ADR). This is a voluntary form of conciliation undertaken before cases are listed for trial. A solicitor contributor to "Viewpoint" in *The Independent* newspaper described this proposal, as it would affect claimants in personal injury cases, as offering a form of inferior justice. The original proposal emanated from the London Common Law and Commercial Bar Association. Under the proposal, if a court decided that a case was suitable for conciliation, the parties would have to attempt it, although the assessments would not be binding. This proposal is seen by the writer in *The Independent* as purely one for reducing delays and cutting costs, taking the view that the prospect of a court trial is the only way to get a fair settlement in a case, especially where the defendant is insured. To extend the scheme beyond commercial disputes and debt cases (to which it is limited in America) would be unjustified in the opinion of many.

Criminal Justice

The extent to which the English legal system is currently undergoing change, and may be poised for further change, may be illustrated by reference to several matters relating to the administration of criminal justice. At institutional level there has been a scrutiny report of the structure and administration of Magistrates' Courts. If the proposals in this report were implemented, Magistrates' clerks would be relieved of much of their purely administrative work and there would be new bodies responsible for the administration of the courts. In the longer term there would be scope for the "rationalisation" of the courts' work and the geographical distribution of courts. With respect to the work of the courts, the Lord Chief Justice has now issued guidelines relating to features in cases of offences triable either way, which justify Crown Court trial. These guidelines follow a report, issued in March 1990, of a working party under Lord Justice Farquharson. The objective is to stop too many cases of a relatively trivial nature going up to the Crown Court. In general terms, either way offences should be tried summarily unless the court considers that the particular case has one or more of the "aggravating features" set out in the guidelines accorded to categories of offence such as burglary, theft, criminal damage, crimes of violence, driving offences and public order offences.

Two further matters impinge on the fundamentals of our system of justice. Hitherto, absolute discretion in sentencing (within the maxima prescribed by statute) has been regarded as an essential element in the independence of the judiciary. There is now provision, of course, for the review of too-lenient sentences (section 36 of the Criminal Justice Act 1988), but in recent months there have been calls for some degree of control over the judges' sentencing powers. There are two reasons for this: a desire to alleviate the overcrowding of prisons by greater use of community service-type orders and a continued search for greater consistency and uniformity in sentencing. Whilst proposals for a sentencing council and the use of non-judicial assessors sitting with a judge, when deciding sentence, have been set on one side, we may expect some firmer guidelines on sentencing to be laid down in a Criminal Justice Bill in the 1990–91 session of Parliament. (The Criminal Bar Association recently proposed a sentencing forum with the Court of Appeal playing a central role in its work). In particular, greater use of sentences which keep the offender in the community will be sought and there is likely to be a general introduction of unit-based fines, related to the resources of the individual after taking account of the individual's essential expenditure. Efforts will be made to reduce the prison population by keeping down the number of people sent to prison for a short period for default in payment of fines.

Finally, disquiet over potential and actual miscarriages of justice has prompted one senior police officer, speaking at the 1990 conference of the Association of Chief Police Officers, to question the use of the adversarial system of criminal justice. He said, "I don't think we always get at the truth in the adversarial system. Pressures which the system creates ... can eventually lead to perjury." It was asserted that, "Courts played to a set of rules that did sometimes result in very bizarre outcomes." In the meantime there is wide support for an independent review body to investigate serious allegations of injustice as well as a further overhaul of the Court of Appeal's powers to set aside convictions or order a re-trial. In the first instance there is a need to convince the judges of the Court of Appeal to use their existing powers more extensively. According to an article in *The Times* (October 8, 1990) there have been only six reported cases since 1969 in which the Court of Appeal has quashed a conviction because of a "lurking doubt." One may question whether, in the light of the Master of the Rolls' comments (noted earlier) about disappointment with a decision not being a sufficient ground of appeal in civil cases, the two divisions of the Court of Appeal place sufficient emphasis on the distinction between "winning on the balance of probabilities" in civil cases and the need for "proof beyond reasonable doubt" in criminal cases.

STATUTORY INTERPRETATION

It must be rare in the annals of Criminal Law that an accused tries to argue that he has committed a serious offence, in order to escape conviction for a lesser offence. Such, however, was the case in *McMONAGLE* v. *WESTMINSTER CITY COUNCIL* [1990] 2 W.L.R. 823, which raised an interesting problem of statutory interpretation.

The statutory background to the case was as follows. By paragraphs 6 and 20 of Schedule 3 to the Local Government (Miscellaneous Provisions) Act 1982, it is an offence for a person to knowingly use premises as a sex establishment without a licence. Schedule 3 applies to the geographical area of any local authority which resolves to adopt it. The Greater London Council (General Powers) Act 1986 enacted that a London borough council which had adopted Schedule 3 to the Act of 1982 could adopt as applicable to their area, the amendent to Schedule 3 as provided in section 12(4) of the Act of 1986. Westminster City Council had so done. By section 12(4) a further category of sex establishment was introduced, termed a "sex encounter establishment." The following definition of sex encounter establishment was added to Schedule 3, in paragraph 3A, and provides, *inter alia*, that such means ... " (c) premises at which entertainments which *are not unlawful* are provided ... " (*italics added*).

A further provision of relevance was paragraph 1 of Schedule 3 which provides: "Nothing in this Schedule—(a) shall afford a defence to a charge in respect of any offence at common law or under an enactment other than this Schedule ... "

In the present case the appellant was convicted of using premises as a "sex encounter establishment" without a licence. It was established that at such premises a peep show machine was operated which allowed customers upon insertion of money into the machine to observe two naked women displaying themselves in a manifestly immoral manner.

After conviction in the Magistrates' Court, the appellant appealed to the Crown Court, the Divisional Court of the Queen's Bench Division and, finally, to the House of Lords.

The appellant argued that the prosecution, in order to secure his conviction, had to prove that the activities at his premises *were not unlawful*. On this interpretation of the statutory phrase "are not unlawful," the prosecution would have to show affirmatively that the activities at the premises were not so indecent in character as to amount to an offence at common law. Whilst the above statutory offence created by the Act of 1982 was summary and carried a penalty of a substantial fine, the common law offences of public indecency were indictable and carried a penalty of a substantial period of imprisonment. This interpretation, commented Lord Bridge, was startling as the appellant could only be guilty of the summary offence if he had not committed the common law indictable offence.

Lord Bridge commenced his analysis of the statute by looking at the social background against which the legislation providing for the licensing of sex establishments was to be considered. After commenting on the revolution in public attitudes to sexual morality, he explained that the Act of 1982 clearly was aimed at controlling sex establishments and the proliferation of such, which it had been considered impossible to effectively outlaw. In defining sex encounter establishments, the use of the phrase "which are not unlawful" seemed unnecessary when read in conjunction with paragraph 1 of Schedule 3 which clearly indicated that a licence afforded no protection to the licensee in respect of any criminal activity committed in the conduct of the licensed establishment. It was probable that the draftsman by the use of the above phrase was merely emphasising that the grant of a licence for a sex encounter establishment did not give legal authorisation for activities which would otherwise amount to a public indecency offence. If the words were given their literal meaning (that is, the activities must be lawful for the licensing provisions to apply), in his Lordship's view, this would have had the consequence of substantially frustrating the primary purpose of the provisions relating to sex encounter establishments. In consequence, to give effect to the intention of the legislature, it was necessary to avoid the absurdity created by a literal interpretation of the words "which are not unlawful," by treating them as mere surplusage. Was this, however, a legitimate exercise of the judicial function, or should the problem created be left to the legislature to remedy?

Whilst his Lordship recognised that there was a strong presumption that every word in a statute must be given some meaning, courts, in the past, had been driven to disregard particular words or phrases when, by giving effect to them, the operation of the statute would be rendered insensible, absurd or ineffective to achieve its evident purpose. Relying upon *Salmon* v. *Duncombe* (1886) 11 App.Cas. 627, in which Lord Hobhouse said:

> "It is, however, a very serious matter to hold that when the main object of a statute is clear, it shall be reduced to a nullity by the draftsman's unskilfulness or ignorance of the law. It may be necessary for a court of justice to come to such a conclusion, but their Lordships hold that nothing can justify it except necessity or the absolute intractability of the language used."

Lord Bridge concluded that it was permissible to treat the words "which are not unlawful" as mere surplusage in order to avoid the substantial frustration of the legislative object. The appeal was dismissed.

It can be seen that this case raised the perennial problem of the limits of the judicial function *vis-à-vis* the legislative supremacy of Parliament. Clearly this is a matter of degree. For a more acute example of this problem, see *Royal College of Nursing* v. *Department of Health and Social Security* [1981] 1 All E.R. 545. Given that the words of the statute made plain the object to be achieved, common sense would seems to suggest that this should not be defeated by further words which were the product of defective draftsmanship.

A second case, *COMDEL SECURITIES LTD.* v. *SIPOREX TRADE S.A.* [1990] 3 W.L.R. 1, illustrates how a court may construe the words of a statute where there is no ambiguity in its wording but nonetheless a situation has arisen which gives rise to doubt as to the ambit of the provision. In the instant case the issue to be determined by the House of Lords was whether the High Court

had jurisdiction, under section 27 of the Arbitration Act 1950, to
extend the time for the commencement of arbitration proceedings
beyond that allowed by the arbitration agreement where the terms of
the agreement allowed the arbitrator to extend the time limit. Section
27 provides:

> "Where the terms of an agreement to refer future disputes to arbitration provide
> that any claims to which the agreement applies shall be barred unless ...
> proceedings [are] taken within a time fixed by the agreement, and a dispute arises
> to which the agreement applies, [the High Court has a discretion to extend time]."

Did the section apply where a time limit set by the arbitration
agreement could be extended by the arbitrator or only where, under
the terms of the agreement, the time limit is absolute and immutable?
Lord Bridge thought that, if the language used was given its natural
and ordinary meaning, it was apt to cover both situations and
therefore the question to be answered was—should the language be
given such effect or, was there something in the context or in the
discernible policy of the statute which dictated that the language
should be given a restricted or a qualified meaning.

His Lordship traced the legislative history of section 27, which had
re-enacted section 16(6) of the Arbitration Act 1934 (which provision
had followed from the Report of the Committee on the Law of
Arbitration (1927) Cmd. 2817, known as the MacKinnon Report).
The MacKinnon Report seemed to support a construction of section
27 which meant that it only applied where the agreement created an
immutable time limit. Certainly at the time of the Report, short,
fixed limits for commencing proceedings were the norm and it was
not until after the Second World War that there began the practice of
giving the arbitrator the discretion to extend time.

Lord Bridge was of the opinion that such a report was invaluable
as an aid to construction, but that it was one thing to use it to resolve
a real ambiguity in the statutory language and quite another to use it
to cut down the meaning of language that Parliament had used in
implementing the Report's recommendations when the ordinary
meaning of that language was plain. His Lordship continued by
indicating that it was not tenable to argue that the mischief behind
the Act, apparent from the Report, was only to give relief where a
claim was barred by an immutable time limit. He said:

> "When a change in social conditions produces a novel situation, which was not in
> contemplation at the time when a statute was first enacted, there can be no a
> priori assumption that the enactment does not apply to the new circumstances. If
> the language of the enactment is wide enough to extend to those circumstances
> there is no reason why it should be not apply."

In any event, in his Lordship's view, the formulation of the mischief behind section 27 (set out above) was too narrow. The mischief which section 27 was intended to remedy was that of hardship caused by a restrictive contractual time limit. This was to be remedied by affording relief in those circumstances where it was proper that a person should be excused his failure to comply with the time limit. As a consequence, remedying such a mischief was compatible with the broad interpretation of section 27 which resulted in it covering both those agreements containing immutable time limit bars and also those subject to an arbitrator's discretion.

A number of features of this report are worthy of comment. First, note that whilst the mischief rule is, in some ways, the most satisfactory rule of statutory interpretation, its application does not necessarily lead to only one conclusion. There is still an element of discretion in formulating the mischief behind an Act. By leaving aside the fact that the MacKinnon Report was concerned with absolute time bars, the court was able to formulate a mischief which supported the conclusion which a literal interpretation warranted. Secondly, this case illustrates the perennial problem that an Act is a hostage to the future, which may hold situations never contemplated at the time of drafting and parliamentary approval (compare the *Royal College* case, above). Thirdly, Lord Bridge gave guidance as to the way in which a pre-parliamentary report ought to be used. Thus, whilst it may be used to resolve ambiguity in the statutory language, it seems it may not be used to cut down the width of clear statutory words. In short, if the words are clear then they should be given their plain and ordinary meaning.

CHAPTER 6

FAMILY LAW

CHILDREN ACT 1989

The *CHILDREN ACT 1989* received the Royal Assent on November 16, 1989 and it is now known that it will be fully implemented (a few provisions are already in force) in October 1991. Effective implementation of the Act's provisions requires the making of numerous rules and regulations but that this will not cause delay in bringing the remainder of the Act into force on the projected date.

The Act deals comprehensively with both public law (*i.e.* involving local authority intervention) and private law aspects of child law and, in the words of Lord Mackay, is " ... the most comprehensive and far-reaching reform of child law which has come before Parliament in living memory." It stems from a number of sources, including recommendations of the Law Commission in its Report No. 172, *Review of Child Law, Guardianship and Custody (1988)*, the D.H.S.S. *Review of Child Care Law (1985)* culminating in the government White Paper on *The Law on Child Care and Family Services (1987)* (Cmnd. 62), and, to some extent, the Report of the *Inquiry into Child Abuse in Cleveland 1987 (1988)*.

The main criticisms of the existing law relating to the care and upbringing of children have been that it is fragmented across a wide range of statutes and has not always been clear and consistent. Faced with these criticisms, the Act's primary aims are (*per* Brenda Hoggett Q.C., Law Commissioner) to provide a coherent body of law and a consistent set of remedies available in all courts in all proceedings.

The comprehensive and far-reaching nature of the Act is illustrated by the fact that it wholly repeals a number of statutes central to the present law in this area, namely the Guardianship of Minors Act 1971, Guardianship Act 1973, Children Act 1975, Child Care Act and Foster Children Act 1980, and significant parts of the Children and Young Persons Act 1969.

Before examining the main private and public law aspects of the Act, it is of value to be aware of some of the more general principles underpinning them.

Parental Responsibility—The Act signals a change of emphasis from the notion of parental *rights* to parental *responsibilities*, which is declared in section 3(1) to mean "all the rights, duties, powers, responsibilities and authority which by law a parent of a child has in relation to the child and his property." The Act thus provides a welcome change in terminology from rights to responsibilities but recognises the difficulty (if not impossibility) of providing an exhaustive list of such responsibilities. It does, however, confirm that all these matters of parental responsibility are subject to the supervision of the court, section 2(8) providing that a person with parental responsibility is not entitled "to act in any way which would be incompatible with any order made ... under this Act."

Not all parents are automatically accorded parental responsibility: the Act follows the existing law in providing that where the mother and father are married to each other at the time of birth then each shall have parental responsibility but, where not so married, it vests in the mother (section 2(1) & (2)). Unmarried fathers will not, as such, have parental responsibility but can acquire it in one of two ways: first, by court order (section 4(1)(*a*)—replacing the similar provision under section 4 of the Family Law Reform Act 1987), or secondly, by a "parental responsibility agreement" (section 4(1)(*b*)), which must be made in a form to be prescribed by regulations. Generally where more than one person has parental responsibility each may act alone in meeting that responsibility and such responsibility does not cease merely because another person also acquires it (although it will be subject to any court order, which might effectively restrict its exercise).

Welfare Principle—Section 1(1) affirms the principle, presently declared in the Guardianship of Minors Act 1971, that in determining any question with respect to a child's upbringing " ... the child's welfare shall be the court's paramount consideration." Further, section 1(2) states the (perhaps self-evident) principle that "any delay in determining the question is likely to prejudice the welfare of the child" and this is supplemented by section 11 and section 32, which require the court in proceedings for certain private and public law orders to draw up a timetable and give directions to try to ensure adherence to it. In all care and supervision order cases and contested proceedings for a section 8 order (see below) a positive duty is placed on the court by section 1(3) to have regard to a list of specified matters, namely:

(a) the ascertainable wishes and feelings of the child concerned (considered in the light of his age and understanding);

(b)   his physical, emotional and educational needs;

(c)   the likely effect on him of any change in his circumstances;

(d)   his age, sex, background and any characteristics of his which the court considers relevant;

(e)   any harm which he has suffered or is at risk of suffering;

(f)   how capable each of his parents, and any other person in relation to whom the court considers the question to be relevant, is of meeting his needs;

(g)   the range of powers available to the court under this Act in the proceedings in question.

In the main this statutory checklist of factors is derived from case law but section 1(5) adds a new dimension in prohibiting the court from making any order under the Act "unless it considers that doing so would be better for the child than making no order at all." Hence, rather than automatically making an order in respect of children on divorce, a court might recognise that child's welfare might equally be served by not intervening or interfering with existing arrangements.

Non-intervenist policy—The Act seeks to encourage parties to settle their own arrangements in respect of the children concerned. This is illustrated by section 1(5), mentioned above, and also finds expression in relation to statutory provisions relating to arrangements for children on divorce, etc. At present in divorce proceedings the court is, by virtue of section 41 of the Matrimonial Causes Act 1973, under a duty to satisfy itself and to make a declaration to the effect that the arrangements for children of the family are satisfactory (or the best that can be devised in the circumstances, or that it is impracticable for the parties to make such arrangements) before making a decree absolute. The usefulness of the section 41 declaration procedure has been called into question and the new Act substitutes this with a provision requiring the court merely to consider whether it should exercise any of its powers under the Act. Parties will be encouraged to provide joint statements regarding proposed arrangements for children and it may be that the court accepts this without more.

Standardisation of powers—Different orders are available in different courts under the present regime and there are restrictions on who can obtain some orders. The divorce court, for example, has flexible powers to award joint or split custody and access in favour of parents and non-parents whereas, in the magistrates' court, the concepts of legal and actual custody are used and access is not generally available to non-parents. The Act provides a new range of orders to replace custody and access and these will be available, irrespective of the court or proceedings involved, to persons "entitled" to apply or, with the court's leave, any other person.

PRIVATE LAW

In the field of private law, the most important change from a practical point of view is that custody, care and control, custodianship and access orders cease to be available. The existing statutory provisions allowing for these orders are being repealed. In their place the Act provides a new, wider range of orders, which may also serve some of the purposes for which wardship might presently be invoked. These orders under section 8 are: a residence order; a contact order; a prohibited steps order and a specific issue order. They are to be generally available to courts dealing with family matters either in "family proceedings," when they can be made by the court of its own motion, or on application. "Family proceedings" are widely defined to include proceedings under the Children Act 1989, Matrimonial Causes Act 1973, Domestic Violence and Matrimonial Proceedings Act 1976, Adoption Act 1976, Domestic Proceedings and Magistrates' Courts Act 1978, section 1 and section 9 of the Matrimonial Homes Act 1983, Part III of the Matrimonial and Family Proceedings Act 1984, and the inherent jurisdiction of the High Court in relation to children.

A **residence order** settles the arrangements as to the person with whom the child is to live and might be seen as the equivalent of the existing care and control or actual custody order. It can be made to specify that the child is to live part of the time with one person and part with another (section 11(4))—a solution not wholeheartedly approved by the courts in the past—see, for example, *Riley* v. *Riley* [1986] 2 F.L.R. 429. A **contact order** requires the person with whom the child lives to allow the child to visit or stay with the person named in the order or for that person and the child otherwise to have contact with each other. Again, to a large extent, this equates to the existing access order but may be seen as wider than providing "staying or visiting access" in that other forms of contact, for example corresponding by letter or telephoning, are allowed for. While these first two "section 8 orders" may appear to amount to little more than modified custody, care and access orders, the terminology is less emotive and may reduce the bitterness felt by parents who presently resent being "deprived of custody." The **prohibited steps order** is self explanatory in that it prevents a person from taking a step which could be taken by a parent in meeting his parental responsibility for a child, and might be used in exceptional cases where wardship was previously used, for example, to prevent non-therapeutic medical treatment. A **specific issue order**, which gives directions for the purpose of determining a specific question which has arisen or may arise in connection with any aspect of parental responsibility, resembles the provision along similar lines in section 1(3) of the Guardianship Act 1973. It might be used, for example, to resolve a dispute between parents over the education of a child and might also be appropriate in cases previously dealt with in wardship.

Under the present law, the persons who may obtain orders in respect of children are generally restricted to parents, parties to a marriage, grandparents (in the case of access orders in the lower courts) and, in the case of custodianship orders, a range of specified persons. There is no *general* restriction on the persons who may obtain a section 8 order, although some require the leave of the court to make application. Parents, guardians and those who already have a residence order are entitled to apply for any section 8 order (section 10(4)). Certain other persons are entitled to apply for a residence or contact order: namely, a party to the marriage (whether subsisting or not) in relation to a child of the family; a person with whom the child has lived for a period of at least three years within the previous five years; a person who has the consent of the persons in whose favour any residence order is in force, the local authority if the child is in care, or each person with parental responsibility. This latter category of persons would include step-parents and long term foster parents who might previously have been seeking a joint custody order or a custodianship order. Rules of court may enlarge the list of persons entitled to apply for an order (section 10(7)). Persons who are not entitled to apply must obtain leave to do so, as for example local authority foster parents with whom the child has not lived for at least three years, although some restrictions are placed on them applying (section 9(3)). Children themselves may also make application, with leave, provided they have sufficient understanding (section 10(8)). Further restrictions also operate in respect of local authorities and in cases where the child is in care. Local authorities are prevented by section 9(2) from applying for or being granted a residence or contact order—the notion is that they should use care or supervision orders to achieve these ends. Local authorities could, however, seek a prohibited steps or specific issue order—for example to ensure medical treatment for a child not in care (currently wardship might be used). Where the child concerned is actually in local authority care the only section 8 order which can be made is a residence order section 9(1)) and this would have the effect of discharging the care order (section 91(1)). Thus, for example, local authorities would not be able to apply to the court for specific issue orders to obtain approval for decisions they want to make in respect of a child—they are expected to exercise powers vested in them without recourse to the court.

"Family Assistance Orders" are a new species of order, available under section 16. They are only to be made in exceptional cases and, though related, are not simply a replacement for supervision orders in matrimonial proceedings but are designed to assist families on a short-term basis, for example during the transitional period of family breakdown. All parties named in the order must consent and it can endure for a maximum period of six months. The order may require a probation officer or an officer of the local authority (usually this would be a social worker) to be made available to "advise, assist and (where appropriate) befriend" any person named in the order, that is any parent or guardian, the child himself, or any person with whom the child is living or in whose favour a contact order is in force.

PUBLIC LAW

In the public law sphere the changes may be seen as even more fundamental. Local authorities are places under a duty to safeguard and promote the welfare of children "in need" and to promote their upbringing by their families by providing a range and level of services appropriate to the child's needs (section 17). The range of support services is set out in Schedule 2. The notion of voluntary reception into care is retained but the Child Care Act 1980, which provided for this, is completely repealed and replaced by section 20. This requires a local authority to "provide accommodation for" any child who appears to require accommodation as a result of: there being no person who has parental responsibility for him; his being lost or abandoned; or the person who has been caring for him being prevented from providing him with suitable accommodation. The local authority is under a duty to consult with persons with parental responsibility before making decisions with respect to the child (section 22(4)) and persons with parental responsibility can remove the child without the necessity of giving 28 days' notice as at present. Most importantly, local authorities will no longer be able to secure their relationship *vis-à-vis* a child in accommodation by passing a parental rights resolution—the present provision for this, in section 2 of the Child Care Act 1980, being repealed and not replaced. This means that if a local authority considers that it should obtain parental responsibility it will need to apply to the court for a care order.

Compulsory care

By section 31(1) a local authority or authorised person (*i.e.* the N.S.P.C.C. and anyone so authorised by order of the Secretary of State) may apply to the magistrates' family panel (replacing the juvenile court jurisdiction) for a care or supervision order, which can only be made if the court is satisfied "that the child ... is suffering, or is likely to suffer, significant harm ... attributable to—(i) the care ... not being what it would be reasonable to expect a parent to give to him; or (ii) the child being beyond parental control." The restricted grounds for care orders mean they they will no longer be available for non-attendance at school but an "educational supervision order" under section 36 will be a possibility in such circumstances.

A care order gives the local authority parental responsibility and section 33 gives guidance on how this may be exercised. Section 34 deals with the specific issue of contact with children in care and places the local authority under a prima facie duty to allow the child reasonable contact with his parents and other specified persons. All these persons, and anyone else with the court's leave, may apply to the court for an order for contact (section 34(3)). Indeed, a court may make such an order for contact, even without application, at the time of making a care order.

As an alternative to care orders, courts may make supervision orders, the nature of which is set out in section 35 and supplemented by detailed provisions in Schedule 3, Parts I and II.

Interim care and supervision orders are available where the court is satisfied "that there are reasonable grounds for believing" that the grounds for a care order under section 31 exist (section 38). The maximum duration for an interim order is eight weeks initially and four weeks for any subsequent orders.

Discharge of care orders is dealt with by section 39 which does not specify grounds for such and would seem to be something for the court to determine on the basis of the "welfare principle" in section 1.

Protection of Children

Part V of the Act deals with measures to protect children. Notable changes include the abolition of the much criticised "Place of Safety Orders," warrants to rescue children, and the powers of the police to take short-term care of children (although other arrangements are made where police protection is needed—section 46). The principal order in this area will be the "emergency protection order" which is to be available, under section 44, where the court has reasonable cause to fear that the child is "likely to suffer significant harm." Its effect is to authorise removal of the child to accommodation provided by the applicant or retention in such accommodation, and to give parental responsibility to the applicant. The child must, subject to any directions of the court, be allowed reasonable contact with parents and certain other persons, and the nature of the order is indicated by the requirement, in section 44(10), that the child must be returned, or allowed to be removed, where this appears safe for the child. Its temporary nature is further illustrated by the fact that the order initially lasts for a maximum of eight days and is extendable only once (section 45) by a maximum seven days.

Mention can be made at this stage of the new "child assessment order," which can be made where the court is satisfied, *inter alia*, that an assessment of the child's health or development, or of the way in which he has been treated, is required in order to determine whether the child is suffering or likely to suffer significant harm. It may be seen as an alternative or a precursor to an emergency protection order, applicable where there is some doubt about whether the criteria for the latter type of order are met. This order is not to be made if the court finds that there are grounds for an emergency protection order and the court may treat an application for a child assessment order as an application for an emergency protection order (section 43(3) & (4)).

Wardship

The use of the wardship jurisdiction of the courts is restricted by the Act in a number of ways. First, section 7 of the Family Law Reform Act 1969, which empowers the High Court to place a ward of court in the care or under the supervision of the local authority, is to be repealed. Secondly, no application for exercise of the court's inherent jurisdiction with respect to children may be made without leave and, thirdly, the jurisdiction cannot be exercised so as to require a child to be placed in care or to be accommodated by a local authority, or to make a child in care a ward of court, or to confer on a local authority power to decide a question of parental responsibility. Local authorities are thus severely restricted in their use of wardship but others may continue to use it subject to the principles in *A.* v. *Liverpool City Council* [1982] A.C. 363.

The Act's 108 sections and 15 schedules contain numerous other provisions relating to matters such as voluntary homes and organisations, registered children's homes, fostering, child minding and day care, and financial provision for children, coverage of which is not possible in the space available. It will be self-evident that some considerable time and effort on the part of students and practitioners will be needed to get to grips with the changes effected by this important and comprehensive piece of legislation and that this contribution has merely provided an insight into some of the important areas of change. A watching brief should be kept on the rules and regulations being made under the Act.

FINANCIAL PROVISION—LUMP SUM

Should a lump sum award made by a court to a spouse on divorce be based solely upon that spouse's needs and is there a strict formula for calculating the amount of that sum? These questions have received the attention of the courts in recent times in the context of "big money" cases.

As long ago as 1982 in *Preston* v. *Preston* [1981] 3 W.L.R. 619, when the Court of Appeal upheld an award of £500,000 estimated as necessary to generate income of £20,000 net per annum, the court was somewhat critical of the lack of detailed information on the financial implications of a lump sum awarded to provide income for a spouse. Three years later in *DUXBURY* v. *DUXBURY* [1990] 1 All E.R. 77 (a case which was belatedly reported, having been decided in 1985) a computerised calculation (which took into account matters such as life expectancy, inflation, return on investments and income tax) of what amount was needed in order to provide income to meet a wife's needs for life was accepted by the court and a lump sum of £540,000 (calculated to generate £28,000 per annum) awarded. After these cases it was arguable that a maximum figure, allowing for inflation, was emerging as an appropriate lump sum award to meet the needs of a spouse in cases of wealthy families and the *Duxbury* approach was a proper method of calculating it.

The Court of Appeal in *GOJKOVIC* v. *GOJKOVIC* [1990] 2 All E.R. 84 considered these matters in a case concerning a couple who had amassed considerable wealth through the hotel business and the husband's property speculation. The husband's assets totalled about £4 million and the wife was seeking a lump sum of £1 million in order to purchase and run a small hotel. This is what the judge awarded in addition to the transfer to her of a maisonette worth £295,000. It was contended on appeal on behalf of the husband that this sum exceeded the wife's reasonable needs, which could be satisfied by the husband's

offer of £532,000 calculated on the *Duxbury* formulation to provide
an annual income of around £30,000, and that the judge had been
wrong in principle to make an award for the purpose of enabling the
wife to purchase an hotel. Butler-Sloss L.J. rejected an argument that
under the revised form of section 25 of the Matrimonial Causes Act
1973 (including section 25A, as substituted by the Matrimonial and
Family Proceedings Act 1984) the court is limited to providing for a
spouse's self sufficiency. Rather she asserted that factors other than
needs are relevant in assessing a lump sum award, such as
contributions by a spouse to the welfare of the family. The judge in
the instant case, having found that the wife's contributions in building
up the wealth accumulated during the parties' cohabitation and
marriage had been exceptional, had been entitled in her Laydship's
view to arrive at a sum of £1 million—how she chose to use that sum
was a matter for her. Russell L.J. could find no authority that there is
a ceiling which should not be exceeded nor that a particular sum (*e.g.*
£30,000 per annum) is an appropriate award in all cases of millionaire
families. Furthermore, the Court of Appeal saw the *Duxbury*
approach as providing useful guidance for a judge but not as
producing a definitive answer as to the sum to be awarded. The
husband's appeal was accordingly dismissed on the basis that the
judge had not exceeded the generous ambit of disagreement which
would allow an appellate court to interfere.

In *B*. v. *B*. [1990] 1 F.L.R. 20 the family was less wealthy in that
the husband, a farmer, was "worth in the order of £1.959 million"
(inclusive of some £800,000 as a remainderman under his grand-
father's will trusts) while the wife had capital of about £100,000.
There was no problem with realising from the husband's assets a sum
sufficient to meet the wife's claim for ancillary relief on divorce. It
having been agreed that a "clean break" order was appropriate, once
again the question of calculation of the lump sum award arose. Ward
J. accepted that the *Duxbury* approach is a very valuable help
provided it is seen as no more than a tool for the judge's use. In his
opinion the approach has a number of limitations, for example the
uncertainty of predictions upon which it is based and an awareness
that capital needs as well as future living expenses might be relevant,
and should be seen only as a means to an end bearing in mind the
very wide discretion given to the courts under section 25 of the
Matrimonial Causes Act 1973.

On the facts of this particular case, Ward J. concluded that the
wife's income needs from the husband were about £15,000. As to the
precise manner of calculating the lump sum needed to generate this
income, the judge preferred an approach based on investments in

equities and gilts rather than purchase of an index-linked annuity, since the former was a more flexible and realistic option for "many wives in their middle years." Taking a four per cent. return as good enough guidance he arrived at a figure of £245,000. On top of this he judged her housing and other needs (*e.g.* a car) to require some £325,000. The final figure for the lump sum award to the wife was accordingly £570,000.

In summary the courts recognise that a spouse's needs are clearly important in assessing a lump sum award and that the *Duxbury* calculation is useful but they will always retain a discretion to take account of all other relevant factors in a particular case and be free to depart from a sum so calculated.

In the two cases mentioned above involving wealthy families the resources were available to make the order the court considerd appropriate albeit the costs associated with property valuation and other matters would reduce these resources. In *EVANS* v. *EVANS* [1990] 1 W.L.R. 575 the family's resources broadly consisted of two mortgaged properties (which were the parties' respective homes after separation) and the husband's shareholding in a small company, which provided his livelihood. No more than £57,000 could be withdrawn from the company without putting it in jeopardy. The wife had no independent means and wished to remain in the matrimonial home and to be provided with a sum which would put the property into good repair and discharge the mortgage (some £28,700 was needed for this), pay off her debts of £4,000 and provide her with an income. As a result of the wife's claim being conducted with "unmitigated acrimony and bitterness," with protracted inquiries and enormous amounts of documentation "serving little useful purpose," her legal costs amounted to some £25,000. The husband's legal costs were in the region of £35,000 and, in the opinion of Booth J., the husband's assets would not allow him to meet all these sums. She therefore concluded that the wife should not be given the matrimonial home with its associated expenses but that it should be sold and the proceeds of sale (after discharge of mortgage, etc.) paid to the wife so as to provide for alternative accommodation for herself and the children. The Law Society's legal aid charge would not attach to the proceeds of sale of the home since these would be fully required for the purchase of a new home, to which a charge would attach for the outstanding costs. A lump sum of £10,000 in the wife's favour was also ordered (£7,500 of which would go towards discharging her costs), together with periodical payments to the wife of £6,500 per annum for three years (by which time she could be in full time employment) and £1,500 per annum for each child.

Booth J. expressed her grave anxiety about cases such as the present, where the costs were out of all proportion to the available assets and recognised the regret which the parties must feel at the assets being dissipated in this way. With the concurrence of the President of the Family Division, Sir Stephen Brown P., guidelines were laid down by her Ladyship for practitioners preparing cases involving substantial ancillary relief. These included:

> (1) the need to confine affidavit evidence to relevant matters and consolidate inquiries in one questionnaire rather than pursuing them in piecemeal fashion; (2) the desirability of the parties jointly obtaining valuations wherever possible; (3) the desirability of pre-trial review to explore possible settlement and define issues; (4) the need for solicitors to keep clients informed about costs and the effect of the legal aid charge.

It is to be hoped that this guidance will minimise the number of cases where, at the end of it all, the parties will be regretting the unfortunate consequences of having eroded their assets in this fashion.

CUSTODY—WELFARE PRINCIPLE

In resolving disputes regarding the custody or upbringing of a child, the paramount consideration for the court is the welfare of the child (section 1 of the Guardianship of Minors Act 1971). The idea that a parent has "rights" over his/her child should have no bearing on this welfare principle. Two recent cases, however, have focussed on the extent to which the courts accept the general assumption that it is desirable for children to be with their natural parent.

In *RE H (A MINOR: CUSTODY)* [1990] 1 F.L.R. 51 the Court of Appeal was faced with an appeal by the Indian mother of a boy against the decision of the judge that care and control should be ordered in favour of the boy's paternal aunt and uncle. The marriage of the mother to the English father was never very happy and on a visit to India when the boy was two the wife refused to return to England and stayed in India with the boy. The husband, an airline agent, visited at intervals until some two years later when, with the mother's agreement, he brought the boy to be educated in England. Although it seemed that the original intention was for the boy to be cared for by his grandparents, he in fact moved in with his paternal aunt and uncle who had a daughter of about the same age. Despite the father having agreed to return with the boy to India for a summer holiday, this did not take place and the mother did not see him for about nine months. At that time she returned to England because she was concerned for his happiness. Initially she had access but this was stopped by the father after a month or so. The mother started divorce proceedings but by the time the access issue came to be decided a further nine months had elapsed during which time she had not seen the boy. In the proceedings access was immediately ordered in the mother's favour and this continued satisfactorily. When the judge eventually had welfare and other reports he accepted that the mother was a capable, warm and loving parent but also recognised that no complaint could be made of the paternal aunt and uncle within whose family the boy had settled well and was changing from being shy, backward and difficult into a normal schoolboy. On balance the judge found that the present family setting provided best for his future development and that it was in the boy's interest for him to stay where he was and continue his schooling in the care and control of his aunt and uncle. The mother was awarded generous access.

On the mother's appeal, O'Connor L.J. and Sir Roualeyn Cumming-Bruce agreed that the judge had considered all the relevant matters: he had not disregarded "the ordinary position that one would expect the child to live with his mother and be brought up by her," and had dealt with the advantages of family life on the one side and of the natural love and affection which the mother was able to offer. Their Lordships confirmed the view of the judge that this was a case of unusual circumstances where the child had been subjected to a series of alterations in his background and they were unable to say that his decision was plainly wrong: the mother's appeal therefore had to fail.

RE K (A MINOR) (CUSTODY) [1990] 2 F.L.R. 64 provides a contrast to the above case and is worthy of note. Here the mother and father had lived together for some considerable periods of time from around the birth of their son in 1985, in a relationship described as "stormy," until the mother committed suicide at the end of 1988. Thereupon the child went to live with his maternal aunt and uncle and their two children. The 23 year old father saw him regularly and applied in wardship proceedings for care and control, asserting that, as the natural father, he was the best person to bring up the child and could do so satisfactorily with the help of his mother. The evidence accepted by the judge was that the father would be a satisfactory parent but he also recognised that the aunt and uncle would provide an excellent, stable home for the boy. Balancing the advantages of being brought up in an exceptionally good home with a normal, young family against fostering the natural relationship between father and son, the judge concluded that the boy's welfare would be better served by giving care and control to the aunt and uncle.

On the father's appeal Fox L.J. cited statements from a number of cases, notably *Re K D (A Minor)* [1988] A.C. 806, in support of the view that the natural parent is usually the best person to bring up a child and that the courts should be reluctant to control or ignore "the parental right" except when the child's welfare so requires. His opinion was that in concentrating on which party/parties, as between the father and the aunt and uncle, would provide the better home for the boy, the judge had not acted properly: the question was not where the child would get the better home but whether it had been demonstrated that the child's welfare "positively demanded the displacement of the parental right." On this finding that the judge had not directed himself properly, his decision was open to review by the Court of Appeal. Since the father, who had always kept in touch with his son, could provide adequate housing and care for him, Fox L.J. could see no ground for displacing the father from his normal role in the care and upbringing of the child. Waite J. agreed and it followed that the appeal was allowed and care and control given to the father.

These two cases are not easily distinguishable although in *Re K* the child's background had not been as disrupted as that in *Re H*. It might be difficult to predict how a future Court of Appeal would react in borderline cases where, after some disruption, the child concerned has settled in a family for a period longer than in *Re K*. This would be particularly so in the light of the accepted test for appellate intervention set out in *G.* v. *G.* [1985] 1 W.L.R. 647, namely, whether the judge of first instance "has not merely preferred an imperfect solution which is different from an alternative imperfect solution which the Court of Appeal might or would have adopted, but has exceeded the generous ambit within which a reasonable disagreement is possible," in short whether the judge is "plainly wrong."

CHILDREN IN CARE—ACCESS

Under section 12B—C of the Child Care Act 1980, where parental access to a child in local authority care is refused or terminated, the parent must be served notice of such and can respond by seeking an access order from the juvenile court. In *R.* v. *WEST GLAMORGAN COUNTY COUNCIL, EX PARTE T* [1990] 1 F.L.R. 339, this train of events occurred but the mother's application for an access order was refused. Some 21 months later the local authority was approached regarding allowing the mother access but responded by indicating that the child was to be adopted and access would not be in his interest. The mother sought a notice from the local authority under the 1980 Act that access was being refused so that she would then be able to apply again to the juvenile court for an access order. The local authority declined to do this, relying on the earlier notice and juvenile court determination of the matter. An application was made on behalf of the mother for judicial review of the local authority's refusal.

The issue before the court, therefore, was the finality of a section 12B notice and whether there are circumstances when it would be appropriate to serve a fresh notice. Sir Stephen Brown P., while expressing sympathy with the position of the mother, nevertheless agreed with the submissions on behalf of the local authority that the proper statutory steps had been taken by the local authority on the earlier occasion and the 1980 Act does not provide for service of a further notice under section 12B. The mother's application for judicial review was accordingly refused. The court did mention a remedy possibly available to the mother, namely to seek discharge of the care order.

It should be noted that when the Children Act 1989 becomes fully operative the Child Care Act 1980 will be repealed and there will be a presumption in favour of parental contact with children in care. Furthermore, where the court refuses a contact order under that Act, further application can be made after six months have elapsed or earlier with the leave of the court.

CHAPTER 7

LAND

A REAL LIFE INTEREST!

An interesting variation on the theme of acquisition of an interest in the family home has occurred in *UNGURIAN* v. *LESNOFF* [1989] 3 W.L.R. 840, casting doubt on Lord Denning's analysis of Mrs. Evans' right in the well known case of *Binions* v. *Evans* [1972] Ch. 359.

The defendant, of Polish origin, had given up her prospects of a university career and the secure possession of her flat in Poland and had entered into a marriage of convenience in order to ensure entry into England to live with the plaintiff, together with her two sons, as man and wife. The plaintiff bought a house where they all lived for some years until the relationship broke down. The plaintiff left and many years later applied for possession of the house against the defendant whose sons, now mature, had left.

When the house was first acquired the defendant and her sons had carried out repairs, removed fireplaces, partitioned bedrooms and installed a shower although the plaintiff had paid for all the materials.

"In my judgment," said Vinelott J., "the inference to be drawn from the circumstances in which the property was purchased and the subsequent conduct of the parties—the intention to be attributed to them—is that Mrs Lesnoff was to have the right to reside in the house during her life ... [The plaintiff] was providing a house as a home for a woman much younger than himself who would be likely to survive him. I do not think that full effect would be given to this common intention by inferring no more than an irrevocable licence to occupy the house. I think the legal consequences which flow from the intention to be imputed to the parties was that Mr Ungurian held the house on trust to permit Mrs Lesnoff to reside in it during her life unless and until Mr Ungurian, with her consent, sold the property and bought another residence in substitution for it.
If that is the right conclusion, then the house became settled land within the Settled Land Act 1925 and Mrs Lesnoff is a tenant for life entitled to call for execution of a vesting deed and for the appointment of trustees." (p. 855)

Having cited *Bannister* v. *Bannister* [1948] 2 All E.R. 133 and *Binions* v. *Evans* [1972] Ch. 359, the judge then went on to say (p. 857),

"Although, of course, every judgment of Lord Denning is entitled to the greatest respect, I do not find the reasons he gives for the conclusion that the defendant in *Binions* v. *Evans* ... was not a tenant for life persuasive. A person with a right to reside in an estate during his or her life, or for a period determinable on some earlier event, has a life or a determinable life interest as the case may be: see *In re Boyer's Settled Estates* [1916] 2 Ch. 404. The estate is necessarily limited in trust for persons by way of succession ... In my judgment, therefore, Mrs Lesnoff is entitled to a life interest in the house ... and when the property is vested in her, will be entitled to sell it and re-invest the proceeds in the purchase of another house or to enjoy the income from them."

The defendant had claimed she should be entitled to the house absolutely because the plaintiff had promised that he would buy her a house where they could live together or alternatively that she should have a right to occupy for her life, and her counsel had argued that she had at least a beneficial interest in the house commensurate with its increase in value because of the work which she had put into it. The decision of the court gives her the right to live there or to income, which whilst short of the absolute ownership sought could be more beneficial economically than the right based on the "increase in value" for which her counsel had argued.

The trust with the plaintiff as trustee for the defendant's right under the Settled Land Act 1925 appears to be, in Vinelott J.'s opinion, a constructive trust:

"The question is whether these facts and the work subsequently done by Mrs Lesnoff, give rise, either to a constructive trust under which Mrs Lesnoff became entitled to a beneficial interest in the house, or to a licence to reside, or to an estoppel preventing Mr Ungurian from denying her right to reside in the house." (p. 854)

It may be that the use of the verbs "infer" and "impute" in the passage at p. 855, quoted above, leave scope for argument as to whether the trust is really a resulting trust based on a common intention or a constructive trust of the remedial variety which seemed to have received a fatal blow in *Grant* v. *Edwards* [1986] Ch. 638 which Vinelott J. cited at length and seems to have been following.

(This case is also considered in detail under the Trusts section of this edition).

STREET v. *MOUNTFORD*—STILL UNDER ATTACK

Find your exclusive possession and you have a tenant (with few exceptions) appears to be the basic rule of law since *Street* v. *Mountford* [1985] A.C. 809. Establishing when there is exclusive possession and when is there an exception to the above rule are recurrent problems.

In *NUNN* v. *DALRYMPLE* [1989] 21 H.L.R. 569, C.A. the exception appeared to be a family relationship between the parties but the court held that such a relationship does not necessarily negative the existence of a lease.

The defendant tenants had given up a council house to move into accommodation provided for them on an informal basis by their daughter's father-in-law. The move was so that they could be near their daughter.

Before moving in they had renovated the property and although no rent had been agreed before the move the defendants had indicated at the very beginning that they wanted "to rent" and they began to make weekly payments when they took up occupation. These payments had increased a number of times over the years.

The plaintiff, who purchased the property from the father-in-law, sought possession against the defendants as licensees, but was unsuccessful. The important decision of giving up a council tenancy ("we have a case not of people who were homeless and being offered a home, but who were living in a council house," O'Connor L.J. at p. 579) and the early mention of payment were crucial, said the court; a commercial relationship had been intended.

In *CARR GOMM SOCIETY* v. *HAWKINS* (September 5, 1989, Willesden County Court) [1990] 4 C.L. 244 an exception did apply. The plaintiff, a registered charity, had provided exclusive possession of a room to the defendant, at a rent, at a time when he had mental problems. The arrangement was stated to be one of a licence and a welfare officer visited the defendant twice weekly. The Society's aim was to provide accommodation and support for single and lonely people and it had 60 homes in London.

The court held that the nature of the Society and its need to move people on, negatived the presumption of a tenancy and the defendant was merely a licensee within a *Street* v. *Mountford* exception.

Attempts to expressly create non-exclusive occupation agreements so as to avoid *Street* v. *Mountford* have not generally been successful and the assured shorthold tenancy should have now displaced them but inevitably the courts will have to deal with them for some years to come. The message appears to be that the land owner will rarely be successful.

In *ASLAN* v. *MURPHY (NOS. 1 AND 2); DUKE* v. *WYNNE AND ANOTHER* [1990] 1 W.L.R. 766 C.A., the appeal court considered two different agreements for different premises and found them to create tenancies, though at first instance the agreements had been found to create licences. A single written judgment was given covering both cases, "in the hope of assisting [lawyers and county court judges and] ... to reduce the scope for argument as to whether we all mean the same thing." (Lord Donaldson of Lymington M.R. at p. 769).

Agreement no. 1 gave a right to occupy a basement room but denied exclusive occupation of any part, giving only the right in common with other licensees, the owner retaining the keys and the "licensee" (as the agreement described him) to occupy ... "between the hours of midnight and 10.30 a.m. and between noon and midnight, but at no other times, for the purpose of temporary accommodation for the licensee's personal use only ... "

Agreement no. 2 also denied exclusive occupation—this time of a three-bedroom house, the owner reserving the right "to place other person or persons in the premises ... ," the occupier "not to interfere with or change the locks on any part of the premises ... "

Each of the premises were in fact occupied exclusively by the "licensee" and agreement no. 2 provided that "the absence of other occupiers whether permanent or otherwise shall in no circumstances be construed as the grant or creation of an exclusive right of occupation ... "

Surprisingly, perhaps, agreement no 1 had been found at first instance as not a sham arrangement and, although it is not stated that this was argued as regards agreement no. 2, Lord Donaldson M.R. dealt with that aspect thus:

> "Quite apart from labelling, parties may succumb to the temptation to agree to pretend to have particular rights and duties which are not in fact any part of the true bargain. Prima facie, the parties must be taken to mean what they say, but given the pressures on both parties to pretend, albeit for different reasons, the courts would be acting unrealistically if they did not keep a weather eye open for pretences, taking due account of how the parties have acted in performance of their apparent bargain. This identification and exposure of such pretences does not necessarily lead to the conclusion that their agreement is a sham, but only to the conclusion that the terms of the true bargain are not wholly the same as those of the bargain appearing on the face of the agreement. It is the truth rather than the apparent bargain which determines the question 'tenant or lodger?'" (pp. 770, 771).

To pretend to agree does not therefore result in a sham agreement and perhaps that concept, as a result of Lord Donaldson's words, can be regarded now as irrelevant, the "true bargain" being the sole question and, to decide it, the factual situation must be looked at.

In this light, were the provisions in agreement no. 1 for sharing the basement room and depriving the defendant of the right to occupy it for 90 minutes out of each 24 hours, part of the true bargain or merely pretences? His Lordship found them to be mere pretences.

Similarly, in agreement no. 2, as the defendants in fact occupied the whole house the true bargain was that they should be entitled to exclusive possession unless and until the plaintiff wanted to exercise her right to insert someone else as a lodger and, said Lord Donaldson (at p. 775), "If that is the case and, for the time being, they have an entitlement to exclusive occupation, they are tenants and their status cannot at some future date be unilaterally converted into that of lodgers by the owner requiring them to share their occupation: *Antoniades* v. *Villiers* [1990] A.C. 417." On the other hand, he said that if the true bargain is that occupiers are entitled to only a share in the right to occupy (although because there is currently no other occupant they enjoy de facto occupation of the whole premises) then they are merely lodgers. This will still be a very difficult distinction to draw.

On the provisions about keys in each agreement, he said, "Provisions as to keys, if not a pretence which they often are, do not have any magic in themselves. It is not a requirement of a tenancy that the occupier shall have exclusive possession of the keys to the property. What matters is what underlies the provision as to keys." A set of keys may be retained, for example, in order to genuinely provide services. This, he said, might infer a licence but that would be because of the services and not because of the retention of the keys.

Retention of keys was also an issue in *FAMILY HOUSING ASSOCIATION* v. *JONES* [1990] 1 W.L.R. 779, C.A., as was the possibility of one of the exceptions adumbrated in *Street* v. *Mountford*.

The Association had given *de facto* exclusive possession of a flat to the defendant. However, the agreement was expressed to be a licence, giving temporary accommodation but no right to exclusive possession. The agreement provided for a weekly payment. An emergency housing worker of the Association retained a key to the flat, this being the usual practice in such cases so as to give free entry whereby the worker might readily offer support to occupiers of the Association's properties and inspect the state of repair of the properties. If an occupier were not at home when such a worker called the key allowed access, though such access had not been used in this case.

The freehold owner of the property was the local authority which had given a licence to the Association so that the Association could provide temporary housing for homeless families referred to it. This "licence" arrangement does not appear to have been argued as necessarily negativing a lease between the Association and the defendant.

Referring to Lord Donaldson's words regarding keys in *Aslan* v. *Murphy* (see above) and the effect of their retention, Balcombe L.J. said (p. 789) that:

" ... there is a spectrum ranging from tenant at the one end to lodger at the other. Whilst the rights retained by the housing association in the present case may be slightly greater than those usually retained by a landlord under a lease, I entertain no doubt that they fall at the 'tenant' end of the spectrum, not the 'lodger' end."

Slade L.J. agreed that the keys were not decisive " ... when all the other circumstances pointed towards her actually enjoying exclusive possession." (p. 792). He also discussed but did not decide the possibility of the case falling within one of Lord Templeman's exceptions to a tenancy indicated in *Street* v. *Mountford*—that of an object of charity (as in the *Carr Gomm* case above). The defendant paid less than a market rent for the accommodation; she was previously a homeless person and the Association had provided advice and support. These were, he thought, special features which might affect the issue.

In any event, the court acknowledged that even if the defendant had only a licence, the effect of section 79(3) of the Housing Act 1985 was to give her the same security of tenure as if she had been granted a tenancy because of her exclusive occupation, and stated that *Family Housing Association* v. *Miah* (1982) 5 H.L.R. 94 and *Kensington and Chelsea (Royal) L.B.C.* v. *Hayden* (1984) 17 H.L.R. 114 to the contrary (decided on the equivalent provision in the Housing Act 1980) were now incorrect. Balcombe L.J. said (p. 790):

"As it appears to be no longer possible to create a licence granting exclusive occupation of self-contained residential property as a separate dwelling (thus excluding lodger type arrangements) in return for periodical money payments, if [*Miah's* and *Hayden's*] cases remain good law their effect would be to deprive s.79(3) of all operation, save only in respect of licences granted for no consideration. That cannot have been the intention of Parliament. In my judgment, the clear intention behind s.79(3) ... was to prevent local authorities from avoiding the operation of Parts IV and V of the Act by granting, as was then believed to be possible, licences which were in all material respects the same as tenancies but which were nevertheless not tenancies. If *Miah's* case and *Hayden's* case are, as I believe, irreconcilable with *Street* v. *Mountford* and *A.G. Securities* v. *Vaughan*, then we are again bound to refuse to follow them under the second exception to the rule in *Young* v. *Bristol Aeroplane Co. Ltd.* [1944] K.B. 718."

EQUITABLE INTERESTS AND PRIORITIES

Whether a person inhabiting a house which is legally owned by another has an equitable interest in that house and whether such interest is binding on a mortgagee dealing with the legal owner are problems which are frequently aired in the courts. *Unqurian* v. *Lesnoff* (see above) is an example of the former issue. *BARCLAYS BANK PLC* v. *KENNEDY* (1989) 21 H.L.R. 132, C.A. gives an example of the latter. In this case, whether the defendant had an interest in the house, which was registered land, was not at issue. However, the defendant had signed a charge deed at her husband's bank, at his request, and she argued that because of undue influence exerted by her husband as agent for the bank, her equitable interest entitled her to remain in possession as against the bank when it sought to enforce the charge.

Her husband had been pressured into agreeing to guarantee debts of his employer, who was in financial difficulties, and those of the business which he and others, as a consortium, intended to take over. The husband's bank was also the creditor of the employer and the bank's intention, to freeze the employer's account, was putting the husband's employment in jeopardy. The husband arranged with the bank to charge with repayment of the employer's debt, the house which he shared with the defendant but of which he was sole legal owner. He signed the necessary deed, as did the bank manager, just before 3.30 p.m. on a Friday afternoon. The manager then left it to him to discuss the matter with his wife over the weekend, it being the bank's normal routine to require an occupier to execute a charge (no doubt a routine only established since *Williams and Glyns Bank* v. *Boland* [1981] A.C. 487), though the bank did not know whether the defendant actually had any proprietary interest. An arrangement was made with the husband for the wife to execute the charge on the following Monday. The husband did not mention the charge to the defendant until about 3.00 p.m. on the following Monday. He then told her it was merely to secure the employer's borrowings (as he believed) for only four days, after which it was to be paid off by another member of the consortium. She was then rushed to the bank to create the charge before the bank closed at 3.30 p.m. Her signature to the deed was witnessed by a clerk of the bank without any discussion of the deed's effect.

The defendant now alleged that her husband had used undue influence on her in order to obtain execution of the deed and that he had done so when acting as agent for the bank. If this were so her consent could be vitiated, preserving the priority of her overriding interest under section 70(1)(g) of the Land Registration Act 1925 (see *National Westminster Bank plc.* v. *Morgan* [1985] A.C. 686).

The appeal court was unwilling to decide whether there had in fact been undue influence, the evidence before it not being sufficient, but it allowed the defendant's appeal against the finding, at first instance, that the bank was not tainted by the acts of the husband. The judge had decided this on the basis that the bank manager had simply told the husband to go home and discuss the charge with the defendant.

The appeal court found this to be a wrong analysis of the situation. The debt owed by the employer had been unsecured and the bank manager had a real incentive, said the court, to obtain the charge to disembarrass himself of that unsatisfactory situation in which his head office was showing an awkward interest. The execution of the charge by the husband and the manager without the defendant, whose signature the manager regarded as a mere formality and which could be obtained by the husband, clearly inferred that the bank was content to leave things thereafter to the husband and that he was acting as the bank's agent in persuading the defendant to attend the bank and sign. If the husband had used undue influence therefore the bank as principal was tainted by it.

In *ABBEY BUILDING SOCIETY* v. *CANN AND ANOTHER* [1990] 2 W.L.R. 832. The House of Lords was called upon to resolve the same problem of priority of interests and in doing so has killed a nice academic argument and lifted a potential headache for conveyancers.

The Society had lent money to buy a house which was to be owned by the chargee but which, unknown to the Society, would not be occupied by him but by his mother, the first defendant, and the man she subsequently married, the second defendant.

Part of the price for the house had come from the proceeds of sale of another house in which the first defendant had had an equitable right. It was accepted, therefore, that she had an equitable right in the instant property which was registered land.

In the Court of Appeal it had been decided that, assuming the equitable interest, the mother had acquiesced in the charge by her son to the Society by leaving it to him to raise the extra finance needed and had thus given him authority to create a charge having priority to her interest. The House arrived at the same conclusion— that she had no priority—but by a different route. It was considered that there was no *scintilla temporis*, no moment of time (as envisaged in *Church of England Building Society* v. *Piscor* [1954] Ch. 553) between the acquisition by the son of the legal estate and the creation of the charge. There was no gap during which he could become trustee of the legal estate in trust for his mother's equitable right.

"Of course as a matter of legal theory a person cannot charge a legal estate that he does not have, so there is an attractive legal logic in the ratio in *Piskor's* case. Nevertheless, I cannot help feeling that it flies in the face of reality. The reality is that, in the vast majority of cases, the acquisition of the legal estate and the charge are not only precisely simultaneous but indissolubly bound together ... The reality is that a purchaser of land who relies upon a building society or bank loan for the completion of his purchase never in fact acquires anything but an equity of redemption ... " (Lord Oliver at pp. 853, 854).

Piskor's case was therefore wrongly decided and the first defendant did not have an equitable interest when the charge was created.

However, she did have such an interest by the time the charge was lodged for registration as the Land Registry. It was therefore necessary to decide the relevant time for establishing priorities. The first defendant claimed it to be the date of registration (rather than the date of creation) and that on registration of the charge her right was protected as an overriding interest under section 70(1)(*g*) of the 1925 Act.

Again, the House found the argument wanting and found that the time for establishing whether an interest *existed*, in order to establish priorities, was the date of registration of the charge 'or estate against which priority was claimed; but the date for establishing whether that interest was *protected* by actual occupation was the date of transfer or creation of the estate or charge. As the mother's right did not exist when the charge was created it could not therefore be binding on the plaintiff.

The House also, however, went on to discuss the nature of actual occupation under section 70(1)(*g*) and put a lid on the box of minutiae which the first defendant's contention as to its meaning could have released.

The purchase of the property had been completed some 35 minutes after the agents of the first defendant had begun to move her carpets and furniture into the house, the first defendant being abroad at the time. Was such vicarious and momentary occupation "actual occupation."

Lord Oliver said:

> "It is, perhaps, dangerous to suggest any test for what is essentially a question of fact, for 'occupation' is a concept which may have different connotations according to the nature and purpose of the property which is claimed to be occupied. It does not necessarily, I think, involve the personal presence of the person claiming to occupy. The caretaker or the representative of a company can occupy, I should have thought, on behalf of his employer. On the other hand, it does, in my judgment, involve some degree of permanence and continuity which would rule out mere fleeting presence ... of course, in the instant case, there was, no doubt, on the part of the persons involved in moving [the first defendant's] belongings, an intention that they [the person's belongings? *ed.*] would remain there and would render the premises suitable for her ultimate use as a residential occupier. Like the trial judge, however, I am unable to accept that acts of this preparatory character carried out by courtesy of the vendor prior to completion can constitute "actual occupation" for the purposes of section 70(1)(*g*)."

The questions of both existence of an interest and, if so, its priority were at issue before the House of Lords in *LLOYDS BANK PLC* v. *ROSSETT AND ANOTHER* [1990] 2 W.L.R. 867 (see also the

Trusts section of this edition). The Court of Appeal had decided both points in favour of the respondents who claimed the beneficial interest. The House decided the first point in favour of the appellant and therefore found it unnecessary to consider the second.

The Rossetts, husband and wife, wished to buy a house with funds from a trust for the husband's family. The trustees of the fund insisted upon the house being legally in the husband's name alone and this was done. The house required renovation and the husband borrowed money from the appellant bank to meet the cost, charging the house, which was registered land, to the bank without Mrs Rossett's knowledge. The bank now sought possession of the house and Mrs Rossett claimed an equitable interest which was an overriding interest under section 70(1)(g) of the Land Registration Act 1925. She alleged that her interest arose out of an agreement with her husband that she should have one.

Lord Bridge of Harwich said:

> "The question the judge had to determine was whether he could find that before the contract to acquire the property was concluded [the Rossetts] had entered into an agreement, made an arrangement, reached an understanding, or formed a common intention that the beneficial interest in the property would be jointly owned. I do not think it is of importance which of these alternative expressions one uses. Spouses living in amity will not normally think it necessary to formulate or define their respective interests in property in any precise way. The expectation of the parties to every happy marriage is that they will share the practical benefits of occupying the matrimonial home whoever owns it. But this is something quite distinct from sharing the beneficial interests in the property asset which the matrimonial home represents (p. 872) ... Even if there had been the clearest oral agreement between Mr and Mrs Rossett that Mr Rossett was to hold the property in trust for them both as tenants in common, this would, of course have been ineffective since a valid declaration of trust by way of gift of a beneficial interest in land is required by s.53(1) of the Law of Property Act 1925 to be in writing. But if Mrs Rossett had, as pleaded, altered her position in reliance on the agreement this could have given rise to an enforceable interest in her favour by way either of a constructive trust or of a proprietary estoppel." (p. 874)

Mrs. Rossett had assisted in the renovation work by assisting in the planning and obtaining of materials, and by carrying out some decorating and preparing surfaces for decorating. Lord Bridge commented:

> "On our view the monetary value of Mrs Rossett's work expressed as a contribution to a property acquired at a cost exceeding £70,000 must have been so trifling as to be almost de minimis. I should myself have had considerable doubt whether Mrs Rossett's contribution to the work of renovation was sufficient to support a claim to a constructive trust in the absence of writing to satisfy the requirement of section 51 ... even if her husband's intention to make the gift ... had been clearly established or if he had clearly represented to her that that was what he intended." (p. 876)

CHAPTER 8

TORT

NEGLIGENCE—DUTY—PUBLIC POLICY

The precise circumstances in which the principle which precludes civil
proceedings where the claim is founded on an illegal or immoral act
(*ex turpi causa non oritur actio*) applies to an action in tort have
never been clearly defined. The issue arose in *PITTS* v. *HUNT* [1990]
3 W.L.R. 542 where the plaintiff was injured in a collision whilst
travelling as a pillion passenger on a motor-cycle whose rider was
killed. The plaintiff had been drinking with the rider before the
fateful trip and knew that the rider did not hold a driving licence and
was uninsured. Immediately prior to the accident, moreover, the
plaintiff had been encouraging the rider to drive in a reckless and
dangerous manner. The plaintiff's claim against the deceased's
personal representative was dismissed at first instance on the ground
that no duty of care was owed because of the *ex turpi* principle. It
was also held that section 148(3) of the Road Traffic Act 1972 (now
section 149 of the Road Traffic Act 1988), precluded the defence of
volenti non fit injuria, but that the plaintiff was 100 per cent.
contributorily negligent.

The plaintiff's appeal to the Court of Appeal was unanimously
dismissed. On the application of *ex turpi causa* Beldam L.J. thought
that, in view of the pragmatic approach taken by the courts in the
past, it was undesirable to attempt to categorise the degree of gravity
involved in offences, such as would be sufficient to bar the plaintiff's
claim. In the instant case his Lordship held that public policy
precluded the recovery of compensation, having regard to the fact
that the plaintiff had actively encouraged the rider to commit offences
which, had a person other than the rider himself been killed, would
have amounted to manslaughter. Balcombe L.J. concurred with
Mason J. in the Australian case of *Jackson* v. *Harrison* (1978) 138
C.L.R. 438 that:

> " ... the denial of relief should be related not to the illegal character of the
> activity but rather to the character and incidents of the enterprise and to the
> hazards which are necessarily inherent in its execution ... a plaintiff will fail when
> the joint illegal enterprise in which he and the defendant are engaged is such that
> the court cannot determine the particular standard of care to be observed."

His Lordship considered that this approach enabled the court to distinguish between joint illegal enterprises which did not disable the court from assessing the standard of care required (*e.g.* the use of a vehicle by an unlicensed and disqualified driver as in *Jackson* v. *Harrison*), and those where it would be impossible to determine the appropriate standard (*e.g.* the use of a getaway car as in *Ashton* v. *Turner* [1981] Q.B. 137). His Lordship felt that the present case fell within the latter category and concluded that no duty was owed to the plaintiff. Dillon L.J. reached the same conclusion by a slightly different route. He thought that the inherent difficulty involved in grading the illegality according to the degree of moral turpitude would be avoided by drawing a distinction (suggested by Bingham L.J. in *Saunders* v. *Edwards* [1987] 1 W.L.R. 1116) between cases where the plaintiff's action arose directly *ex turpi causa* and those where the plaintiff had suffered a genuine wrong to which the allegedly unlawful conduct was incidental. The plaintiff's action in the present case, said his Lordship, clearly came within the former category so as to defeat the claim.

In considering whether *volenti* afforded a defence to a vehicle driver sued by his passenger their Lordships unanimously agreed that, notwithstanding that the facts might clearly indicate a willing acceptance of the risk of negligence, the effect of section 148(3) of the Road Traffic Act 1972 was to preclude reliance on such a defence. However, Balcombe and Dillon L.JJ. held that the words "agreement or understanding" in that section did not contemplate an illegal agreement, express or tacit, to embark upon an illegal venture, so that the statutory provision did not affect the defence of illegality. Turning finally to the question of contributory negligence, their Lordships considered that the trial judge's finding that the plaintiff was 100 per cent. to blame was logically insupportable. As Beldam L.J. pointed out, section 1(1) of the Law Reform (Contributory Negligence) Act 1945 starts with the initial premise that there is fault by both parties which has caused damage and concludes by saying that the damages recoverable shall be reduced in accordance with the claimant's share in the responsibility for the damage. The statute therefore pre-supposes that the plaintiff will recover some damages and to hold him 100 per cent. responsible is not to hold that he shared in the responsibility for the damage. Leave to appeal was granted.

Similar issues arose in *KIRKHAM* v. *CHIEF CONSTABLE OF THE GREATER MANCHESTER POLICE* [1990] 2 W.L.R. 987. The facts were that the plaintiff's husband was remanded in custody on a charge of criminal damage damage. The police knew of recent attempts by the accused to commit suicide but failed to follow the normal procedure of notifying the prison authorities on a standard form that he fell within the category of prisoners regarded as exceptional risks. While in prison the accused, who had been diagnosed as suffering from clinical depression, committed suicide and, as administratrix of his estate, the plaintiff brought an action in negligence against the police. At first instance Tudor Evans J. found in the plaintiff's favour on the ground that the defendants owed a duty to the deceased, that their breach of duty was an effective cause of his death, and that the *ex turpi* principle had no application. The defendants appealed to the Court of Appeal.

On the question of whether a duty was owed, the defendants had argued, *inter alia*, that the law did not impose liability for pure omissions, relying for this proposition on the speech of Lord Goff in *Smith* v. *Littlewoods Organisation Ltd.* [1987] A.C. 241. The court unanimously dismissed this argument, however, and held that liability would be imposed in respect of an omission where, having regard to the relationship between the parties, the defendant had assumed a responsibility towards the plaintiff and the latter had relied upon the assumption thereof. In these circumstances, said their Lordships, the defendant would come under a duty to speak and, in the present case, by taking the accused into custody the defendants assumed the responsibility to him of passing to the prison authorities information which might affect his well-being, and reliance upon that assumption by the accused could readily be inferred. The police were therefore held to owe a duty of care of which they were in breach by failing to forward the relevant information. Their Lordships further accepted the trial judge's finding that, on the balance of probabilities, the accused would have been prevented from taking his own life had the authorities been aware of the risk, and thus held that the breach was the cause of the damage.

Having established liability the court had then to consider whether the defendants could rely upon a defence of *volenti non fit injuria* or upon the *ex turpi* maxim. Their Lordships rejected the first alternative on the ground that, notwithstanding that the suicide was a conscious and deliberate act, medical evidence indicated that the accused was clinically depressed and could therefore not properly be regarded as *volens*. Farquharson L.J. decided the issue on the additional ground that the defence was inappropriate where the act of the deceased was the very occurrence which the duty cast upon the defendant required him to prevent. Lloyd L.J. was not as sanguine in his approach and said that the defence would apply in the case of a person of sound mind, although he accepted that unsoundness of mind did not necessarily connote insanity in the legal sense.

As far as the *ex turpi* principle was concerned, Tudor Evans J. had taken the view that this defence depended upon some causally related criminal activity and could therefore not apply since the abolition, in 1961, of suicide as a crime (section 1 of the Suicide Act 1961). Lloyd L.J., however, said that recent cases had made it apparent that the defence was not confined to criminal conduct, but rather depended for its operation upon whether to afford relief would affront the public conscience; and Farquharson L.J. observed that the essence of the principle was that no action would lie if it was based on immoral conduct. It was unanimously held that, having regard to the fact that the public attitude to suicide had changed from one of abhorrence towards one of sympathy (as evidenced by the 1961 Act), and to the fact that a much greater understanding of mental instability had been achieved with the development of medical science, it could not be said that an action brought in respect of a suicide (or attempted suicide) was grounded in immorality or would affront the ordinary citizen. The defence therefore failed, Sir Denys Buckley adding that he was not satisfied that a dependant's claim for compensation under the Fatal Accidents Act 1976 could ever be adversely affected by turpitude on the part of the deceased. Leave to appeal was refused.

NEGLIGENCE—*VOLENTI NON FIT INJURIA*

It is rare indeed that the defence of *volenti* will succeed in a negligence action, since it is a requirement that the plaintiff not only has full knowledge and appreciation of the nature and extent of the risk, but that he also voluntarily agrees (expressly or by implication) to incur it, thus effectively waiving his right of legal action. In *MORRIS* v. *MURRAY AND ANOTHER* (*The Times*, September 18, 1990) the plaintiff and the deceased agreed, after a prolonged drinking bout together, to go on a flight in the deceased's aircraft. Flying conditions were poor, the runway was wet and uphill, and the deceased took off downwind when, in the opinion of an expert, he should have taken off on a different runway and into the wind. After climbing to about 300 feet the aircraft stalled and dived into the ground, severely injuring the plaintiff. In the plaintiff's action for negligence against the administrators of the pilot's estate, the judge, at first instance, rejected a plea of *volenti* but accepted a defence of contributory negligence and reduced the damages by 20 per cent.

The Court of Appeal unanimously upheld the defendants' appeal. Fox L.J. referred to *Dann* v. *Hamilton* [1939] 1 K.B. 509, in which *volenti* was held not to apply to a claim by a passenger in a motor vehicle whose driver was drunk. Although the decision had been the subject of much criticism it was approved by the Court of Appeal in *Slater* v. *Clay Cross Co. Ltd.* [1956] 2 Q.B. 264, but his Lordship did not consider that approval as going beyond the decision on its facts. In *Dann* the plaintiff had been on an ordinary social outing with a driver who was sober at the start and who did not become drunk until it was time for the return journey, when it would have been difficult for the plaintiff to extricate herself without giving offence. Those facts, said his Lordship, bore little resemblance to the situation in the instant case where it was plain from the evidence that the plaintiff knew that he was going on a flight with the deceased as pilot and that the deceased had been drinking heavily. Although the plaintiff's evidence was that he would not have embarked on the flight had he been sober that did not, according to Fox L.J., establish that he was in fact incapable of understanding what he was doing. It was therefore held that, by embarking on such a wildly irresponsible venture, the plaintiff had knowingly and willingly accepted the risks and had thereby implicitly waived his rights in the event of injury consequent on the deceased's failure to fly with reasonable care; furthermore, there were no considerations of policy for reaching a different conclusion.

NEGLIGENCE—DUTY—ECONOMIC LOSS

Where a dangerous defect in a chattel is discovered before it causes any personal injury or damage to property (*i.e.* property other than the defective chattel itself), the defect is one merely of quality. In other words the chattel is either capable of repair at economic cost or is worthless and must be scrapped, but in either case the loss sustained is purely economic. While such loss is recoverable against a party who owes the loser a relevant contractual obligation, it is not recoverable in tort in the absence of a special relationship of proximity imposing upon the tortfeasor a duty of care to avoid causing economic loss. As a general rule there is no such relationship between the manufacturer of a chattel and a remote owner or hirer. These fundamental propositions appeared to have been modified in the case of defective buildings by the decisions in *Dutton* v. *Bognor Regis Urban District Council* [1972] 1 Q.B. 373 and *Anns* v. *Merton London Borough Council* [1978] A.C. 728. In the latter case, the assumed facts of which were similar to *Dutton*, it was held that a local authority could owe a common law duty of care in respect of its statutory powers of inspection under the Public Health Act 1936, though only in so far as the defect constituted a present or imminent danger to the health or safety of the occupants of the building. Notwithstanding that Lord Denning in *Dutton* and Lord Wilberforce in *Anns* characterised the loss as physical damage to the building, the inescapable conclusion is that in both cases the loss was purely economic in the sense that the plaintiff had merely received less than he bargained for.

It is clear, then, that *Dutton* and *Anns* represented a departure from established principle and the high-water mark came with *Junior Books Ltd.* v. *Veitchi Co. Ltd.* [1983] 1 A.C. 520 in which the House of Lords made an unambiguous attempt to establish a general duty of care in respect of pure economic loss. That case was, however, assiduously distinguished on a number of occasions by the Court of Appeal on the ground, *inter alia*, that to impose a duty in tort without reference to a carefully constructed chain of contractual relationships would make a mockery of contractual negotiations (see, e.g. *Simaan General Contracting Co.* v. *Pilkington Glass Ltd. (No. 2)* [1988] Q.B. 758; *Greater Nottingham Co-operative Society Ltd.* v. *Cementation Piling and Foundations Ltd.* [1988] 3 W.L.R. 396). There can no longer be any doubt that the decision in *Junior Books* is restricted to the particular facts of the case. Furthermore, certain observations in *D. & F. Estates Ltd.* v. *Church Commissioners for England* [1988] 3 W.L.R. 368, notably of Lords Bridge and Oliver, cast doubt upon *Dutton* and *Anns*, and the whole issue of liability for defective buildings recently came before the House of Lords in *MURPHY* v. *BRENTWOOD DISTRICT COUNCIL* [1990] 3 W.L.R. 414.

The facts of *Murphy* were that the appellant council referred the plans for the building of a house to consulting engineers acting as independent contractors, pursuant to its duty under section 64 of the Public Health Act 1936. The engineers' report failed to take note of calculation errors in the design of the foundation, but the council approved the plans in reliance upon the report with the result that the house was built with defective foundations. During the plaintiff's occupation of the house the foundations cracked and caused extensive damage to the walls and pipes of the building. The plaintiff did not carry out repairs, estimated at £45,000, but sold the house for £35,000 less than its market value in undamaged condition and claimed damages for negligence against the council. Both at first instance and in the Court of Appeal it was held that the statutory duty imposed on the council could not be discharged by delegating its performance to independent contractors so that, by relying on the negligent advice of the engineers, the council had itself been negligent. Since the defects constituted an imminent danger to the plaintiff's health and safety it was therefore held, applying *Anns*, that the plaintiff acquired a cause of action to recover the amount of expenditure necessary to eliminate the danger. The council appealed to the House of Lords.

A unanimous House consisting of seven Lords of Appeal invoked the *Practice Direction of 1966* and, overruling *Anns*, held that where a defect in a building was discovered before any personal injury or damage to property other than the defective house itself had been done, the expense incurred by the building owner in rectifying the defect was pure economic loss and therefore irrecoverable in tort. Lord Keith accepted the proposition that a careless builder would be liable, in accordance with the principle in *Donoghue* v. *Stevenson* [1932] A.C. 562, where a latent defect caused physical injury to any person, be they owner, occupier, visitor or passer-by, or to the property of any such person. But, said his Lordship, it was equally clear that a person who was injured through consuming or using a product of the defective nature of which he was well aware had no remedy against the manufacturer, so there could likewise be no liability towards an occupier who knew the full extent of the defect yet continued to occupy the building. Furthermore, he said, there was no liability in tort upon a manufacturer towards the purchaser from a retailer of an article which turns out to be useless or valueless as a result of careless manufacture, and it was difficult to draw a distinction between an article which is useless or valueless and one which suffers from a defect which would render it dangerous in use but which is discovered by the purchaser in time to avert the possibility of injury. In these circumstances the purchaser could either incur expense in rectifying the defect or he could discard the article, but in either case the loss was purely economic.

Having thus classified the true nature of the loss held to be recoverable in *Anns*, Lord Keith turned to a consideration of whether the local authority owed a duty of care not to cause pure economic loss to the plaintiff and concluded that it did not. His Lordship's reasoning was that to hold otherwise would necessarily lead to the imposition of a similar duty upon the builder, in which case there would be no grounds in logic or in principle for not extending liability to the ordinary manufacturer of a chattel, and to do so would be to " ... open on an exceedingly wide field of claims, involving the introduction of something in the nature of a transmissible warranty of quality." It would, moreover, be open to question whether any distinction ought to be drawn between chattels which are dangerously defective and those which are merely rendered useless by reason of the alleged defect. Describing the decision in *Anns* as a "remarkable example of judicial legislation" his Lordship said that it had the effect of imposing upon builders a liability going far beyond that which Parliament saw fit to impose by the Defective Premises Act 1972, and he expressed support for the view that, in what is essentially a consumer protection field, the precise extent of the liabilities which in the public interest should be imposed upon builders and local authorities is best left to the legislature.

In a concurring speech Lord Bridge endorsed the view in *Anns* and *Dutton* that the negligent performance by a local authority of its statutory functions could attract no greater liability than that attached to the negligence of the builder, but he was not convinced that its potential liability in tort was necessarily co-extensive with that of the builder. He referred to his suggestion in *D. & F. Estates Ltd.* v. *Church Commissioners for England* [1989] A.C. 177 that in the case of a complex structure such as a building, one element of the structure might be regarded, for the purposes of the *Donoghue* v. *Stevenson* principle, as distinct from another element, so that damage to one part of the structure caused by a hidden defect in another part might fall to be treated as damage to "other property." On closer analysis his Lordship reached the conclusion, as did Lord Keith, that the "complex structure" theory was unrealistic because the structural elements in any building formed a single indivisible unit of which the different parts were essentially interdependent. However, he continued, there was a critical distinction between a structural element which was dangerous only because it did not perform its proper function of sustaining the other elements, and a distinct item incorporated in the structure which positively malfunctioned, thereby causing damage to that structure. His Lordship then gave the example of a defective central heating boiler which exploded and damaged a house and said that damages would be recoverable on *Donoghue* v. *Stevenson* principles. In less forceful terms Lord Keith expressed a similar sentiment.

Lord Bridge next considered the requirement in *Anns* that there be present or imminent danger to the health or safety of the occupiers of the building and pointed out that this gave rise to insurmountable difficulties. For example, he said, a latent defect which was not discovered until it caused the sudden and total collapse of a building at a time when the building was temporarily unoccupied and which caused no damage other than to the building itself would give rise to no cause of action, whereas if the defect had become known before the collapse of the building the local authority would be liable for the full cost of repair.

In his Lordship's view the above considerations led to the inevitable conclusion that the negligent performance by a local authority of its statutory functions of approval or inspection would enable a building owner to recover the cost of repair only if the duty incumbent upon the authority was sufficiently wide to encompass economic loss. Having regard to section 1 of the Defective Premises Act 1972, which imposed upon builders obligations amounting to a transmissible warranty of the quality of their work, his Lordship said that it would be "remarkable" if similar obligations, applicable to buildings of every kind and subject to no such limitations or exclusions as were imposed by the 1972 Act, could be derived from the builder's common law duty of care or from any duty imposed by building regulations. It therefore followed that the local authority incurred no liability because, although a builder could be liable to a building owner for pure economic loss in those exceptional circumstances where there existed between them a special relationship of proximity sufficiently akin to contract to import the *Hedley Byrne* principle of reliance (and *Junior Books* could only be understood on this basis), no such relationship ordinarily existed between the authority and the purchaser of a defective building.

Lord Oliver, too, thought that the liability of the local authority was not logically separable from that of the builder. For the same reasons given by Lord Bridge he rejected the "complex structure" theory and said that the crucial issue was not the nature of the damage *per se*, but whether the scope of the duty of care in the particular circumstances was wide enough to embrace damage of the kind which the plaintiff was alleged to have suffered. He said that in the context of the infliction of direct physical injury by the defendant's act there was no need to look beyond Lord Atkin's concept of reasonable foresight of harm in order to establish the requisite degree of proximity, but in the case of economic loss foreseeability alone was insufficient. His Lordship then reasoned that if the manufacturer of a defective chattel owed no duty to an ultimate consumer in respect of economic loss, a builder could owe no such duty to a remote building owner and, *a fortiori*, the local authority could not be liable for failing to prevent the builder from inflicting pecuniary loss by conduct which was not itself tortious.

Lord Mackay L.C. and Lord Jauncey expressed views in sympathy with those of Lords Keith, Bridge and Oliver. Lord Brandon concurred with Lord Keith, and Lord Ackner with Lords Keith, Bridge, Oliver and Jauncey. Three further points which remain unresolved by the House are worthy of note. First, although Lords Keith and Oliver adverted to the question whether, assuming the council was under a duty, it discharged that duty by acting on the advice of apparently competent consulting engineers, neither thought it necessary to determine the point. Secondly, their Lordships left open the question whether a local authority would owe a duty to an occupier who suffered personal injury (or, presumably, damage to property) as a result of its failure to take reasonable care in securing compliance with building regulations. Counsel for the authority had accepted that such a duty did exist, but none of their Lordships was prepared to concede that such was necessarily the case. Finally Lord Bridge, with whom Lord Ackner agreed, thought that where, after discovery of a dangerous defect, a building remained a potential source of injury to persons or property on neighbouring land or on the highway, the owner ought in principle to be able to recover in tort from the negligent builder the cost necessarily incurred in order to protect himself from his potential liability to third parties. Lord Oliver was unconvinced by this argument but reserved his opinion on the matter.

NEGLIGENCE—ECONOMIC LOSS AGAIN

One practical effect of *Murphy* v. *Brentwood District Council* will be to stem the tide of litigation in respect of defective buildings. Even before that decision the courts had succeeded in confining *Anns* within reasonable bounds by a careful process of distinguishing. In *RICHARDSON* v. *WEST LINDSEY DISTRICT COUNCIL* [1990] 1 W.L.R. 522 the Court of Appeal held, dismissing the plaintiff's appeal, that in the exercise of its supervisory functions over building operations a local authority owed no duty of care to an original building owner, save in exceptional circumstances. Their Lordships appeared to acknowledge a distinction between pure economic loss and risk to health and safety, but in any event held the distinction to be immaterial because it was normally incumbent upon the building owner himself to ensure that the building was erected in accordance with the relevant building regulations. It is now clear from *Murphy*, however, that in so far as expense is incurred in eliminating the risk to health or safety, no such distinction exists, so that the plaintiff will presumably not now be pursuing his appeal, leave for which was granted by the Appeal Committee.

In *DEPARTMENT OF THE ENVIRONMENT* v. *THOMAS BATES AND SON LTD.* [1990] 3 W.L.R. 457 the plaintiffs were occupiers of a building which they discovered was supported by concrete pillars which were insufficient to carry the design load. In an action against the defendants for the cost incurred in having the pillars strengthened, the judge at first instance and the Court of

Appeal dismissed the claim on the ground that the *Anns* principle did not apply because, inasmuch as the building could continue to be used safely as long as there was no increase in the load, there could not be said to be an imminent threat to health or safety. The plaintiffs' appeal came before the House of Lords shortly after *Murphy*, and inevitably, it was unanimously dismissed.

As far as defective construction work is concerned we now have a much clearer idea of what constitutes damage for the purposes of a successful tort action. In other cases the courts have been equally reluctant to entertain claims for pure economic loss. Thus, in *Reid* v. *Rush & Tomkins Group plc* [1989] 3 All E.R. 229 the Court of Appeal held that the common law duty owed by an employer did not import any obligation either to provide personal accident insurance or to advise the employee to obtain such cover against certain risks arising from a posting abroad, so as to protect the employee from financial loss. Similarly, in *VAN OPPEN* v. *CLERK TO THE BEDFORD CHARITY TRUSTEES* [1990] 1 W.L.R. 235 a school was held to be under no duty to have regard to its pupils' economic welfare by advising on the dangers inherent in a game of rugby football or to take out personal accident insurance. It therefore followed that the school could not be said voluntarily to have assumed a duty to advise parents on the question of insurance.

Where the plaintiff suffers economic loss as a result of reliance upon a negligent misstatement his claim will succeed provided that the principles established in *Hedley Byrne & Co. Ltd.* v. *Heller & Partners Ltd.* [1964] A.C. 465 are satisfied. In *Caparo Industries plc* v. *Dickman and Others* [1990] 2 W.L.R. 358 (see the Company Law section of this edition) the House of Lords held that, in making their report in compliance with the Companies Act 1985, the defendant auditors owed no duty of care to the plaintiffs either as existing shareholders in the company whose accounts the defendants had audited or in their capacity as non-shareholding buyers. Their Lordships indicated that liability under *Hedley Byrne* was confined to situations where the maker of the statement was, or ought to have been, aware that his advice or information would in fact be made available to, and be relied upon by, a particular person or class of persons for the purposes of a particular transaction or type of transaction. Since the purpose of the statutory audit was to make a report to enable the shareholders to exercise their powers in general meeting and not to provide information to assist them in making investment decisions, the defendants owed no duty of care. As far as non-shareholding investors were concerned it was further held that there was no reason in policy or principle why the defendants should be considered as having a special relationship with them, not-withstanding that the defendants should have known that the affairs of the company were such as to render it susceptible to an attempted takeover.

In view of the above it will come as no surprise to learn that a company auditor owes no duty of care to existing or potential creditors of the company. Millett J. had so decided in *AL SAUDI BANQUE* v. *CLARKE PIXLEY* [1990] 2 W.L.R. 344 which the House of Lords approved. Whilst *Caparo* may not be particularly remarkable for what it actually decides, it has, like *Murphy*, potentially far-reaching implications for the future development of negligence as a tort. Gone are the halcyon days of the post-*Anns* era when the courts came to equate proximity with foreseeability for the purposes of establishing the existence of a duty of care. In their place came Lord Keith with his insistence that foreseeability of harm was but the first, albeit a necessary, step in the equation. The net result of recent judicial activity is that, in considering the issue of duty or no duty, one must look to the type of harm which the plaintiff is alleged to have suffered. It has already been noted that where the defendant's act causes direct physical harm Lord Oliver in *Murphy* suggested that one need look no further than the neighbour principle to establish the requisite degree of proximity. However, as Lord Bridge remarked in *Caparo*, it is one thing to owe a duty of care to avoid causing injury to the person or property of others, but it is quite another to avoid causing economic loss. His Lordship said that, while it was important to recognise the underlying general principles common to the whole field of negligence, the law had moved in the direction of attaching greater significance to the more traditional categorisation of distinct and recognisable duty situations. He then cited with approval the following dictum of Brennan J. in the Australian case of *Sutherland Shire Council* v. *Heyman* (1985) 60 A.L.R. 1;

> "It is preferable, in my view, that the law should develop novel categories of negligence incrementally and by analogy with established categories, rather than by a massive extension of a prima facie duty of care restrained only by indefinable 'considerations which ought to negative, or to reduce or limit the scope of the duty or the class of persons to whom it is owed.' "

Lords Roskill, Oliver and Ackner concurred, thus sounding the final death-knell of the Wilberforce two-stage test in *Anns*.

CHAPTER 9

TRUSTS

TRUSTS—CONSTITUTION—*DONATIO MORTIS CAUSA*

As the students of Trusts knows well, a trust must be completely constituted, either by effective declaration of trust or transfer of the trust property to trustees. Nevertheless the courts will enforce a valid contract to create a trust. One of the exceptions to the rule that Equity will not perfect an imperfect gift (*i.e.* will not enforce an agreement to create a trust in the absence of a valid contract) is the *donatio mortis causa*. Thus, in the case of the *donatio mortis causa*, or "death bed gift," on the death of the donor, Equity will compel the donor's Personal Representatives (Executors or Administrators) to perfect the gift by transferring the property in question to the donee.

It has always been said, following dicta of Lord Eldon in *Duffield* v. *Elwes* (1827) 1 Bli.(N.S.) 497, that there cannot be a valid *donatio* of land, although Professor Pettit in *Equity and the Law of Trusts* (6th ed.), p. 105 doubts this view. However, the point was directly considered for the first time in *SEN* v. *HEADLEY* [1990] 1 All E.R. 898. The donor, who was in hospital suffering from terminal cancer, said that he gave his house and contents to the donee, that the title deeds of the house were in a steel box and that the donee had the key (which he had slipped into the donee's handbag). The donor died three days later. The donee subsequently went to the house, took the deeds from the box, and sued the estate for a formal conveyance of the house.

The three criteria for a valid *donatio* were set out by Farwell J. in *Re Craven's Estate* [1937] Ch. 423. It was held that the first two were satisfied, namely a clear intention to give, in the event of the donor's death, and that the gift was in contemplation of the donor's impending death. The third criterion, that the donor had parted with dominion of the property, posed the difficulty, since it requires that the donor must put it beyond his power to substitute other assets for those given.

In the case of a *donatio* of personal property, it has been held in *Re Lillingston* [1952] W.N. 338 that handing over the only key to a locked box will suffice to part with dominion of the assets contained in the box, since the donor will no longer have access to them, and title to the assets passes on delivery. In the instant case, the court declined to extend this principle to land, because such authorities as there were did not favour this approach. Crucially, statute demands formality for the transfer of land (sections 52 and 53 of the Law of Property Act 1925). As a result, the mere parting with possession of the title deeds does not result in parting with the dominion of the land. The title deeds relate to the earlier dealings with the land, and do not entitle the person holding them to claim the land in the absence of a conveyance or declaration of trust in his favour. Indeed, it would still be possible for the donor to execute a conveyance or declaration of trust in favour of another.

DUTY OF SELLING TRUSTEE

Buttle v. *Saunders* [1950] W.N. 255 confirms that the duty of a trustee in selling assets on behalf of the trust is to obtain the best price he can in the interests of the beneficiaries. This duty is amplified by the statement of Sir George Jessell M.R. in *Re Cooper and Allen's Contract for Sale to Harlech* (1876) 4 Ch. 802 that: "It is their duty to sell the estate to the best advantage of the beneficiaries. If the sale can be at a higher price by joining with another, they are performing this duty by obtaining that higher price." The question of whether this duty may in some way be limited was considered in *SERGEANT* v. *NATIONAL WESTMINSTER BANK PLC* [1990] 59 P. & C.R. 182, where the trustees would have been placed in a considerable dilemma had the joinder principle been applied.

The defendants and their brother had held the freehold of their deceased father's three farms as trustees under his will. The defendants had been granted yearly agricultural tenancies by their father and were executors and residuary beneficiaries of his will. The plaintiffs were the executors of the defendants' brother, who had been a tenant, executor and beneficiary along with the defendants. The plaintiffs' claim was that the farms be sold, and that the defendants owed a duty as trustees, not only to obtain the best price but also as tenants to join in the sale to enable an enhanced price by reason of vacant possession to be obtained. It was pointed out, in support of the claim, that it was common practice for a landlord seeking to sell the freehold to negotiate with his tenants for them to vacate the property, on the basis that the sale proceeds be divided, perhaps 50/50. It was decided, however, that despite the normal rules relating to the duties of trustees, set out above, the defendants' duty was simply to sell most advantageously that which they held *in their capacity as trustees*. As tenants, they owed no duty to sell, or even to be reasonable in accepting any offer made to them, and in any event, it would be highly artificial and unsatisfactory to create a duty to negotiate with themselves.

It is most likely, however, that this is a limited exception to the general rule, created because the rule, if applied, would have deprived the trustees of their livelihood.

RESULTING TRUST—CONTRIBUTION TO PURCHASE

When a person claims an interest in property which is in the name of another, it is vital to the success of the claim to establish a common intention of the parties that such an interest be created. It should be recalled that the trust so created ought, correctly, to be described as a resulting trust (since it is intended by the parties), but that it will on occasion be described as a constructive trust by the courts. The importance of establishing a common intention in such cases has been emphasised in a series of recent cases.

In *Howard* v. *Jones* (1989) 19 F.L.R. 231, it was decided that the absence of such an intention was fatal to the plaintiff's claim, even if some contributions had been made to the purchase, unless the circumstances gave rise to an estoppel. If a contribution had been made, that may justify a finding of implied intention to create a trust. On the facts, there was neither a substantial contribution nor an intention to create a trust.

On similar facts, in *WINDELER* v. *WHITEHALL* (1990) 154 J.P. 29, the same conclusion was reached for similar reasons, save that the court accepted the possibility that indirect contribution to the purchase may suffice, such as doing unpaid work for the property owner, thereby freeing his income to pay the mortgage. It was pointed out that the fact that parties decide to cohabit does not indicate that they therefore intend to alter their property rights.

The same issue was considered again in the House of Lords decision in *LLOYDS BANK PLC* v. *ROSSET* [1990] 1 All E.R. 1111. As in the cases previously mentioned, the plaintiff's case was relatively weak. A married couple had purchased, in the husband's name only, a somewhat dilapidated property. The wife had performed certain tasks in order to prepare the house for occupation—namely instructing builders and co-ordinating their work, obtaining materials for the builders and delivering them to the site, using her professional skills to help the husband plan the renovations and decorations, papering two bedrooms and preparing four rooms for papering. The purchase was funded by a trust fund, the trustees of which would only advance the money if the house was to be in the

husband's sole name. This fact made it impossible for the House of
Lords to find a common intention that the wife should have a
beneficial interest. In any event it was felt that clear evidence would
be needed to establish such an intention where, as here, the wife's
contribution was of small value in relation to the value of the
improved property. The work was regarded as being such as any wife
would undertake in her husband's absence in order to make the
house habitable by Christmas.

Their Lordships considered that a common intention may be
evidenced by express discussion between the parties, which will
normally precede or coincide with the purchase. In such cases, the
party seeking to establish a trust must then show that he acted to his
detriment or irrevocably altered his position. If, on the other hand,
there was no express intention, the court may infer a common
intention from contribution to the purchase or mortgage. It was felt
that nothing less than financial contribution would suffice. The
reasoning adopted by the court in *Grant* v. *Edwards* [1986] Ch. 638
was approved and adopted.

One may wonder whether this decision affects the standing of the
decisions in *Eves* v. *Eves* [1975] 1 W.L.R. 1338 where no direct
contribution was made to the purchase of the property, however, that
decision was approved on the basis that there was an express
common intention. It should also be noted that in cases where there
is an express common intention, the court may well award the
plaintiff a larger share than the value of his or her contributions
would otherwise merit.

A case which does not fit easily into the above analysis is
UNGURIAN v. *LESNOFF* [1989] 3 W.L.R. 840, where a common
intention was inferred from the circumstances, rather than from
express discussions, and there was no direct financial contribution.
However, it must be said that the circumstances did point to some
intention to create a trust. The defendant, who was Polish, and the
plaintiff, who was Lebanese and much older and wealthier, decided
to set up house in London. The plaintiff also had homes in other
countries. The house was purchased in the plaintiff's name only, and
was to be occupied by the parties, the defendant's two children and
one of the plaintiff's children. The defendant gave up a promising
academic career and a flat in Poland which was of superior standard
and was hers for life. She only gave up the flat once the London
house had been purchased. The defendant carried out substantial
work on the property—re-wiring, plumbing, redecorating, installing a
shower, and partitioning the bedrooms. The plaintiff sought
possession after the relationship had broken down and the children
had left home.

The court relied on *Grant* v. *Edwards* to decide that a beneficial interest was intended by the parties, despite the fact that there was no direct evidence of intention, merely inference from the circumstances. The decision in *Eves* v. *Eves* was relied on to show that there had been an indirect contribution to the purchase through the improvements. It was held that the terms of the trust were that the defendant was entitled to a life interest in the house, to equate with the security of tenure which she would have enjoyed had she remained in Poland. It should be noted that the trust was described as constructive, and that once again, the size of the defendant's share bore no relation to the value of her contributions. Also, although the rules concerning whether a constructive or resulting trust will arise are now more settled than they have been for some time, there is still some willingness to vary them slightly in order to do justice as between the parties.

(This case is also considered under the Land Law section of this edition).

CONSTRUCTIVE TRUST—STRANGERS TO TRUST—KNOWING RECEIPT—KNOWING ASSISTANCE

A stranger to a trust can become subject to a constructive trust when he either knowingly receives trust funds or knowingly assists the trustees in a breach of trust. The courts have recently had to consider the meaning of the word "knowingly" in each of these two situations.

The first case, *LIPKIN GORMAN* v. *KARPNALE LTD.* [1989] 1 W.L.R. 1340, involved knowing assistance in a breach of trust. A partner in the plaintiff firm of solicitors was, without his partners' knowledge, a compulsive gambler. He drew over £200,000 from the firm's Client account, needless to say without his partners' knowledge, to fund his gambling habit. The bank manager became aware of the solicitor's gambling habit, did not believe the solicitor's statement that it was controlled and knew that substantial sums had been drawn from the firm's Client account. Nevertheless, he did not stop the use of the Client account or inform the firm. It was therefore alleged that the bank was a constructive trustee on the basis of knowing assistance, under the principle in *Barnes* v. *Addy* (1874) 9 Ch.App. 244.

This provides that anyone who assists with knowledge a dishonest or fraudulent design on the part of trustees is liable to be treated as a constructive trustee.

The difficult question has always been as to the degree of knowledge on the part of the third party which is required in order to invoke the rule. Five degrees of knowledge were set out by Peter

Gibson J. in *Baden Delvaux & Lecuit* v. *Société Générale pour Favoriser le Developpement du Commerce et de l'Industrie en France SA* [1983] B.C.L.C. 325, namely:

(i)   actual knowledge;

(ii) wilfully shutting one's eyes to the obvious;

(iii) wilfully and recklessly failing to make the inquiries which a reasonable man would have made;

(iv) knowledge of circumstances which would indicate the facts to an honest and reasonable man; and

(v)   knowledge of facts which would put an honest and reasonable man on inquiry.

It was suggested by Ungoed-Thomas J. in *Selangor United Rubber Estates Ltd.* v. *Craddock (No. 3)* [1968] 1 W.L.R. 1555, and supported in *Karak Rubber Co. Ltd.* v. *Burden (No. 2)* [1972] 1 W.L.R. 602, that what was required on the part of the third party or stranger in order to hold him liable as constructive trustee in a dishonest and fraudulent design was:

> "knowledge of circumstances which would indicate to an honest, reasonable man that such a design was being committed or would put him on inquiry, which the stranger failed to make, whether it was being committed."

The view was taken by Sachs L.J. in *Carl Zeiss Stiftung* v. *Herbert Smith & Co. (No. 2)* [1969] 2 Ch. 276 that this statement was too wide, and that what was required was an "element ... of dishonesty or consciously acting improperly as opposed to an innocent failure ... to make proper inquiry." This view was approved in the instant case, and the correctness of the views expressed in *Selangor United Rubber* v. *Craddock* and *Karak Rubber Co.* v. *Burden* was doubted. It was felt that nothing less than a want of probity was required to found liability, even though it would not always suffice. The view was also taken that only the first three categories of knowledge set out in *Baden* would suffice.

It was further indicated that often, in such cases, a claim of negligence is also made against the alleged constructive trustee. However, the view was taken that the duty to inquire into known facts in relation to potential liability as a constructive trustee should not be equated with any duty to inquire to avoid liability for negligence. To do otherwise would muddy the waters in applying the *Baden* test, and it was felt that this confusion led to the error in the *Selangor* and *Karak* cases. Applying the test, the bank escaped liability because the manager was not party to the solicitor's dishonesty, nor was he wilful or reckless as to what occurred. There was no real reason to suppose that the solicitor was using the funds for his own purposes.

The second case, which deals with liability as a constructive trustee for knowing receipt and knowing assistance is *AGIP (AFRICA) '.TD.* v. *JACKSON* [1989] 3 W.L.R. 1367. This case also considers ι ιe law on "tracing" and this matter is considered as a distinct issue ')elow).

The plaintiff company's chief accountant altered a payment order for over $500,000 to the name of a certain company. The money was transferred from the plaintiff company's Tunis bank account via New York to the payee company's London bank account. The first and third defendants were the directors of the payee company. After the paying bank had tried to recall the payment, the payee company was wound up, the account closed, and the moneys transferred to an accountancy firm called Jackson & Co., the partners of which were the first and second defendants and of which the third defendant was an employee. The money was then transferred by Jackson & Co. to the Isle of Man, and thence to persons abroad. Each of these transfers by Jackson & Co. was in accordance with clients' instructions.

AGIP, the plaintiff company, attempted to trace as much as possible of the missing money, but to the extent that the attempt was unsuccessful, it was alleged that the defendants were constructive trustees of the money and had acted in breach of trust. It was not alleged that the defendants were parties to the fraud or that they had actual knowledge of the fraud. The defendants pleaded that they had at all times acted in accordance with their clients' instructions.

First, it was considered whether liability would exist as a result of their knowing receipt of trust funds. It was held that a trust was imposed on the recipient if he received the money for his own benefit and had actual or constructive knowledge that it was trust property and that the transfer was in breach of trust, either at the time or subsequently, or he received the property lawfully and for another, but later misappropriated it or dealt with it inconsistently with the trust. In neither case was it necessary to know the full terms of the trust, nor was it necessary that the breach of trust be fraudulent. Applying this test, none of the defendants was liable, since one had no knowledge of the breach of trust and the others did not receive any money for their own use and benefit.

Then, the question of knowing assistance was considered. It was held, following *Belmont Finance Corporation Ltd.* v. *Williams Furniture Ltd.* [1979] Ch. 250 that, in this situation, the breach of trust must be fraudulent and dishonest. So far as the third party is concerned, actual knowledge of the breach will always suffice to found liability. No view was expressed on the suggestion in *Re Montagu's Settlement Trusts* [1987] Ch. 264 that constructive notice may not suffice, even in knowing receipt cases, while it clearly is insufficient in knowing assistance cases. The court went on to depart from the views expressed in *Baden* in three respects.

First, it was felt that the view expressed in *Baden*, that the same test of knowledge should apply to knowing receipt cases as to knowing assistance cases, was not necessarily correct, because tracing and knowing receipt cases involve issues of priorities, whereas knowing assistance cases are concerned with participation in fraud. It may therefore be justifiable to have differing standards of knowledge applying to the two situations. In knowing assistance cases, it was considered that what was required was dishonest furtherance of a dishonest scheme. It would clearly be illogical to require a lesser test of knowledge for the assistant than for the principal.

Secondly, it was felt that the accepted view that knowledge in *Baden* categories (iv) and (v) would not suffice to found liability was too much of a generalisation. The view was taken that it was theoretically possible that knowledge in those categories would amount to more than constructive notice. The true distinction was between honesty and dishonesty. If the defendant suspected nothing or his suspicions were allayed, he would escape liability. If he suspected something, but felt it was none of his business, or he did not want to know whether something was amiss, liability would ensue as if he had had actual knowledge.

Finally, it was stated in *Baden* that to escape liability, the plaintiff must show that inquiries would have revealed the truth, on the grounds that a causal connection must be established between the failure to inquire and the loss. This approach was felt to be incorrect in that the basis of liability is the constructive trustee's failure to be honest. It was felt to be probably incorrect in relation to constructive notice also. It would be unreal to speculate whether plausible excuses could be invented to explain what had happened. The liability is imposed for assistance in the fraudulent breach, not for the failure to inquire, which is merely evidence of dishonesty.

On the facts, the defendants were held liable as constructive trustees, because they were concealing the destination of the money from the plaintiffs, and made no inquiries because they thought it none of their business. They were indifferent to fraud, failed to act honestly and participated in the misapplication of trust funds. The first and third defendants knowingly assisted in the breach, and the second defendant was vicariously liable for the first and third, who were his partner and employee respectively.

TRACING—THIRD PARTIES—COMMON LAW AND EQUITY

In the case of *AGIP (AFRICA) Ltd.* v. *JACKSON* [1989] 3 W.L.R. 1367, the facts of which are given above (see Constructive Trust), the court had to consider whether it was possible to trace missing money into the hands of the recipient firm.

It was decided that, at common law, the nature of a tracing action is for money had and received, and that therefore an original recipient of the money remains liable even after parting with the money and despite the fact that there is no impropriety on the part of the recipient. This contrasts with the standard textbook view (see Pettit, *Equity and the Law of Trusts* (6th ed.), pp. 451–452) that the common law tracing remedy does depend on the continuing possession of the assets concerned.

In the instant case the court considered that there were two circumstances which could have defeated the common law claim—the mixing of the money with other money before receipt by the defendants, and the fact that the defendants (the accountancy firm) held the money as agents. Mixing by the defendants, by paying the money into their firm's bank account, would be irrelevant, however, if it occurred after they had notice of the plaintiff's claim. It was held that *Banque Belge pour l'Etranger* v. *Hambrouck* [1921] 1 K.B. 321 was authority for the proposition that a subsequent transferee, such as the defendants, may be liable to account at common law, but only if: (a) the money was acquired other than for value; (b) the money was still held; and (c) there was no question of mixing. On the present facts, however, the defendants had held the money as agents. Thus, once they had accounted to their principal, the tracing action could be brought against the principal only, provided that the fact of the agency and the identity of the principal had been known to the plaintiff, and the accounting to the principal took place before the claim was known to the agents. There would be no defence to an agent, however, if he were implicated in his principal's fraud.

On the facts, the court indicated, it was not established that the claim was known to the defendants before any mixing occurred, but merely that the paying bank had attempted to recover the payment. In any event, as liability was not dependent on the continued possession of the funds, mixing by the defendants was irrelevant. Mixing by a prior recipient, however, would be fatal to a claim, because it would then be impossible to prove that the defendant had ever been the recipient of the plaintiff's money; tracing at common law, said the court, serving an evidential purpose.

The transfer of funds had been made through the international banking system, whereby mere instructions are transmitted from bank to bank rather than money. As Millett J. put it, "Nothing passed between Tunisia and London but a stream of electrons." No common law tracing of money into the hands of the defendants was therefore possible and the defendants were not liable on that score, said the court. In addition, the accounting by the defendants to their principal before they had notice of the plaintiff's claim defeated any common law tracing.

In equity, however, money can be traced through bank accounts but, in order to trace, there must be a fiduciary relationship—*Re Diplock* [1948] Ch. 466, though the court doubted the correctness of this rule without deciding the point. Such a relationship, said the court, must be between the payer of the money and its owner or arise between the payee of the money and the owner by virtue of the payment. On the facts, there was indeed a fiduciary relationship between the plaintiff company and its employee who had perpetrated the fraud. A third party such as the defendants dealing with such a fiduciary must account unless he receives the money as a bona fide purchaser without notice of the impropriety, though a volunteer need not account if he has parted with the money without prior knowledge of the trust.

It was therefore held that any money which remained in the defendants' possession after receipt of knowledge of the fraud must be accounted for, but that they could not be liable for money received and disposed of without notice of any breach of the fiduciary relationship.

RESULTING TRUST—PURCHASE OF PROPERTY IN THE NAME OF ANOTHER

When property is purchased in the name of another, a resulting trust is presumed in favour of the purchaser. If this presumption is to apply, the evidence must show an intention to advance the money, rather than to create a loan. In the latter case the person making the loan would be a mere creditor.

A recent example of this principle is provided by the case of *SEKHON* v. *ALISSA* [1989] 2 F.L.R. 94. A mother and daughter decided to purchase a house for £36,500. The mother paid £21,500 from her savings, and the balance was obtained by mortgage for which the daughter was to be responsible since she was in work. The house was conveyed into the daughter's name only. A few years later, the house was converted into flats, and the upper flat was treated as belonging to the mother, and the lower as belonging to the daughter. The daughter alleged that the house was a gift to her, subject to a moral obligation to return the mother's contribution. It was held that this was not so, because the evidence indicated that the mother saw the purchase as a type of investment and that, at one stage, the daughter accounted to the mother for part of the rent of one flat.

On the basis that an investment was intended, it was possible that the contribution was a loan or a resulting trust. It was held that a resulting trust was intended, because there was a presumption to that effect and evidence that the mother expected to be paid back was not inconsistent with a resulting trust.

An odd footnote to this decision is that, although it was held that equitable interests in proportion to the contributions of the parties came into existence at the time of the conveyance to the daughter, the size of the mother's interest was limited to the value of the upstairs flat. The court therefore awarded her a lease of the flat, to satisfy her equitable interest. This approach would appear to be inconsistent with decisions, such as *Turton* v. *Turton* [1988] Ch. 542, which decide that the size of the equitable interests of the parties is decided at the time of acquisition of the property and cannot be altered by subsequent events, such as separation of the parties.

INDEX